MW00354507

Issuer Perspectives on Securitization

Edited by

Frank J. Fabozzi, Ph.D., CFA

WILEY

John Wiley & Sons, Inc.

Cover Design

There are two photographs that appear on the cover of this book. The top photograph was obtained from the Bermuda Department of Tourism. The bottom photograph was obtained from Alan Benoit Photography, 1101 E. Mesquite Street, Gilbert, AZ 85296. COPYRIGHT 1998 ALAN BENOIT PHO-TOGRAPHY. We thank both the Bermuda Department of Tourism and Alan Benoit Photography for permission to use the photographs.

Table of Contents

Contributing Authors

Len Blum	Prudential Securities Inc.
Karen Cook	Bankers Trust Company
Chris DiAngelo	Dewey Ballantine
Mahesh K. Kotecha	MBIA and CapMAC Asia
Michael A. Mattera	Prudential Securities Inc.
James E. Myers	Lewtan Technologies, Inc.
W. Alexander Roever	First Chicago Capital Markets, Inc.
Marty Rosenblatt	Deloitte & Touche LLP
F. Jim Della Sala	Bankers Trust Company
Michael J. P. Selby	Imperial College of Science, Technology and Medicine and The University of Warwick
Andrew A. Silver	Moody's Investors Service
Joseph D. Smallman	Vining-Sparks IBG

Chapter 1

The Joy of Securitization: Understanding Securitization and its Appeal

W. Alexander Roever, CFA
Director, Head of ABS Research
First Chicago Capital Markets, Inc.

INTRODUCTION

Since the mid-1980s, securitization has grown in importance as a funding strategy for banks and finance companies and has more recently proven an attractive source of funds for other types of firms as well. The increased popularity of this financial tool can be demonstrated by the rapid growth of the markets for asset-backed securities (ABS) and asset-backed commercial paper (ABCP) — the two principal sources of funds for securitization. According to the Federal Reserve, the outstanding balance of ABS grew over 200% between 1991 and the first quarter of 1998 (see Exhibit 1). Outstanding ABCP grew an even more astonishing 635% over the same period. Excluding the market for agency-backed mortgages, over $1 trillion of debt backed by securitized assets were outstanding as of March 31, 1998.

WHY SECURITIZE?

Securitization appeals to a broad range of companies, large and small, in many different industries. To grasp why it has gained in popularity as a financing alternative, it helps to have an understanding of the many advantages securitization provides relative to more traditional sources of funding such as bank lines or corporate debt. The more significant advantages of securitization include:

The author thanks Carol Oliver and Ruth Leung of First Chicago Capital Markets, Inc. for their assistance in preparing this chapter.

1

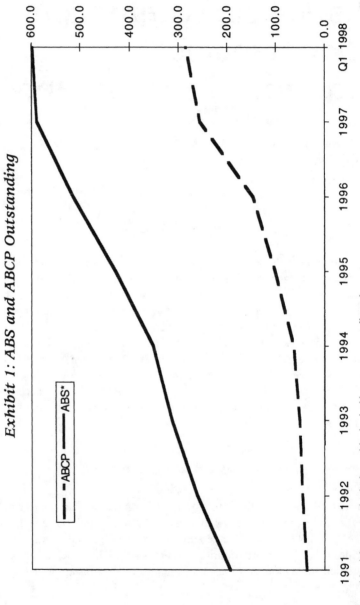

Exhibit 1: ABS and ABCP Outstanding

* Includes residential mortgage backed securities backed by non-agency collateral.

Source: First Chicago Capital Markets, based on Federal Reserve Board estimates.

Lower cost of funds. Financial assets with predictable payment characteristics can, when pooled together, offer a more attractive risk and return profile than the credit of the company that originated them. Many financial assets can be used to structure securities of higher credit quality, and lower cost, than the originating company could issue on its own. Through securitization, a non-investment grade company can often finance itself at investment grade rates.

Source of liquidity. Historically, the ability of small- and medium-sized firms to grow has been constrained by their limited ability to borrow from traditional sources. Because securitization provides a reliable and relatively unconstrained source of off-balance-sheet financing, it mitigates traditional funding constraints, and can promote a company's growth.

Diversified funding source. The use of securitization has not been limited to small or non-investment grade firms. To the contrary, many large, highly rated companies rely on securitization in conjunction with other forms of borrowing, as a means diversifying their funding sources.

Earnings acceleration and management. Current U.S. GAAP accounting allows originators to realize significant accounting gains at the time of securitization. SFAS 125[1] requires securitizing firms to realize an accounting gain at the time of securitization equal to the present value of excess servicing, a practice that accelerates the recognition of income relative to non-securitizers. For companies that securitize regularly these gains are an important source of income and a powerful tool for earnings management.

Off-balance sheet financing. Most securitizations transfer assets and liabilities off-balance sheet, thereby reducing the amount of the originator's on-balance sheet leverage. This off-balance-sheet financing can help improve the securitizer's ROE and other key financial ratios.

Less public disclosure than competing methods of financing. For privately held or non-US firms, securitization provides a means of financing that does not require complete financial disclosure to investors, rating agencies or regulatory authorities, as more direct forms of financing often do. Even for publicly issued ABS transactions, issuer disclosure requirements are less than those required for other kinds of SEC registered securities. In securitization analytical scrutiny is shifted from the company to the structure of the transaction, the characteristics of the underlying assets and the ability of the company (or its surrogate) to service the assets.

---

[1] Statement of Financial Accounting Standards Number 125, *Accounting for Transfers and Servicing of Financial Assets and Extinguishment of Liabilities.* See Chapter 7 of this book for a discussion of FASB 125.

WHAT IS SECURITIZATION?

Securitization is a form of financing where monetary assets with predictable cash flows are pooled and sold to a specially created third party, which has borrowed money to finance the purchase. These borrowed funds are raised through the sale of asset-backed securities, which can take the form of either commercial paper or bonds.

Although it may share passing similarities with older types of financing such as secured lending and factoring, securitization differs in several important respects. A concept central to securitization is that the cash flow generated by a company's financial assets can be used to support one or more securities which are, on average, of higher credit quality than the company itself. To achieve this higher credit quality, the securities used to fund the securitization rely on the cash flow created by the assets, and not on the payment promise of the company. This contrasts with secured lending, where repayment depends primarily on the company's willingness and ability to pay, and only secondarily on the liquidation value of the collateral.

Because both involve the sale of receivables, securitization is often compared to factoring. But, factoring involves recourse to the seller and transfers of customer control from the seller to the factor, that do not occur with securitization. In addition, although traditional factoring provides liquidity to the seller, it does not as securitization does, accelerate the receipt of cash flow or earnings.

WHAT DOES IT TAKE TO SECURITIZE?

The creation of securities that can rely on the cash flows created by a given set of assets requires that the owners of the securities have a claim of the highest priority against the assets. This claim needs to be established in such a way that the assets are protected against tax or other governmental liens that might arise against the selling company in the normal course of business, or from the demands of the originating firm's creditors in the event of its bankruptcy. Although bankruptcy is not a concern if the seller is a bank or thrift, the potential for insolvency and receivership create concerns that closely parallel those of bankruptcy.

In a typical securitization, the segregation of these risks from the assets is accomplished by their sale from the company to a specially created corporation or trust, often called a *Special Purpose Entity* (SPE). SPEs are intended to be "bankruptcy remote" — a term which means that SPEs are legally organized, and their activities are limited, such that the probability of their ever becoming entangled in a seller's potential bankruptcy, or entering into bankruptcy themselves, is extremely low.

Once the SPE has been established, the assets can be transferred from the seller to the SPE by means of a "true sale at law" — that is, a sale executed on an arm's-length basis that effectively conveys ownership of the assets for bankruptcy purposes. Failure of a transfer to be characterized as a true sale by a bankruptcy court could result in the voiding of the sale, and it instead being deemed a secured financing. This could put the assets in jeopardy, and could result in payment delays and possibly losses to the owners of the ABS. To provide supporting evidence of the nature of the sale, counsel on behalf of the seller will provide a true-sale opinion, opining to the intent and character of the sale.

In addition to meeting stringent legal requirements, securitizations must also be constructed to address certain accounting and tax issues. Chief among the accounting issues is whether the financing meets the requirements for off-balance-sheet treatment. Generally, an asset transfer that is a true sale for legal purposes will qualify for off-balance sheet treatment if the SPE acquiring the assets is legally independent of the seller. However, if the SPE is a wholly owned subsidiary of the seller, U.S. GAAP would normally require the assets of the SPE to be consolidated on the seller's balance sheet.

On the tax side, several issues must be addressed in any securitization. One of the most important concerns the sale of the assets and whether it constitutes a taxable event for the seller. Depending on the seller's particular situation, a degree of latitude may exist allowing for a sale to be classified either as a sale or as a financing for tax purposes. How a transaction is classified for tax purposes is independent of its treatment for either bankruptcy or accounting purposes. Therefore it is possible, and indeed quite normal, to have a securitization structured as a sale for bankruptcy purposes and as debt of the seller for tax purposes. For instance, by structuring a securitization such that the ABS qualify as debt of the seller for tax purposes, it is possible to avoid paying taxes that might be incurred if the financing were instead structured as a sale of assets. Just as a true sale opinion is required for bankruptcy purposes, a tax opinion from recognized tax counsel is needed to support the desired tax treatment.

The second major tax issue is whether the SPE itself is subject to taxation. Because the sole purpose of a securitization SPE is to buy and hold assets until they liquidate, SPEs have no outside source of income. Introduction of an entity-level tax would render most securitizations uneconomic. Fortunately, there are several methods of avoiding an entity level tax. The particular method most often depends on the legal form of the SPE.

A common form of SPE, the *grantor trust*, is a passive tax vehicle, allowing all of its income and expenses to flow through to investors. While the grantor trust provides a clear solution for the problem of entity taxes, they also have operational constraints that limit them to issuing only a single senior interest in passthrough certificates. *Passthrough securities* are those that promptly pass principal and interest collections through to investors.

Other SPE types including *limited liability corporations, owners trusts, master trusts* overcome many of the limitations of grantor trusts. These SPEs are sometimes referred to as *paythrough structures*, have an ability to modify the flow of cash and therefore can issue highly structured securities. Unlike grantor trusts, these other SPE types are often incorporated in structures that avoid taxation by using an SPE that qualifies as a subsidiary of the seller for tax purposes. As a precautionary step, SPE organizational documentation usually contains a provision that the entity will convert to a partnership if tax authorities determine that the SPE is taxable. Similar to grantor trusts, partnerships typically pass income and expenses through to their partners.

Under certain circumstances, SPEs may be able to address the entity level tax issue by electing and qualifying for status as a *Real Estate Mortgage Investment Conduit* (REMIC) or *Financial Asset Securitization Investment Trust* (FASIT). By electing status as a REMIC or a FASIT, a trust can avoid entity level taxation without having to have a back-up partnership arrangement in place. However, use of a REMIC or a FASIT is subject to a variety of constraints and limitations. REMICs have been used extensively in the securitization of mortgage assets, but their use is limited strictly to mortgages or other assets secured by real property. Although FASITs can be used to securitize both mortgage and non-mortgage assets, they have been used little since their introduction in 1996. One of the major factors discouraging their application is that gains incurred on the sale of assets into the FASIT are normally taxable at the time of sale.

Clearly, many issues must be addressed when structuring an effective securitization. Exhibit 2 provides a simplified example of how bankruptcy, accounting, and tax issues might be dealt with in a single securitization. The structure depicted uses two SPEs to create a transaction that provides the seller with off-balance-sheet financing while simultaneously protecting the transferred assets from the risk of a seller's bankruptcy and avoiding a federally taxable asset sale. SPE A is organized as a wholly owned, bankruptcy remote subsidiary of the seller, and the assets are transferred to the SPE via a true sale. The combination of the true sale of assets and SPE A's bankruptcy remoteness are intended to put the assets beyond the reach of the seller, or the seller's creditors. Although a sale has taken place for bankruptcy purposes, SPE A's status as a wholly owned subsidiary should cause the SPE to be consolidated with the seller for federal tax purposes. As a result, the transfer from the seller to SPE A should not be considered taxable under federal law.[2]

Using only the structure outlined so far, SPE A could issue ABS to fund its purchase of the assets. However, GAAP would require that any debt issued by SPE A be recorded on the seller's balance sheet. Alternatively, the seller could achieve off-balance sheet treatment by using a second entity, SPE B, as the ABS issuer. To gain this desired accounting treatment, SPE B should be organized as an independent bankruptcy remote entity, and the transfer of assets from SPE A should be structured as a sale for accounting purposes and a financing for tax purposes. SPE B's legal form (e.g., owner trust, master trust, etc.) is likely to be driven more by economic than other considerations.

---

[2] A comprehensive discussion of the legal and other aspects of two-tiered securitizations can be found in Steven L. Schwartz, *Structured Finance: A Guide to the Principles of Asset Securitization, Second Edition* (New York: Practising Law Institute, 1993), pp. 21-48.

Exhibit 2: A Two-Tiered Term Securitization Structure

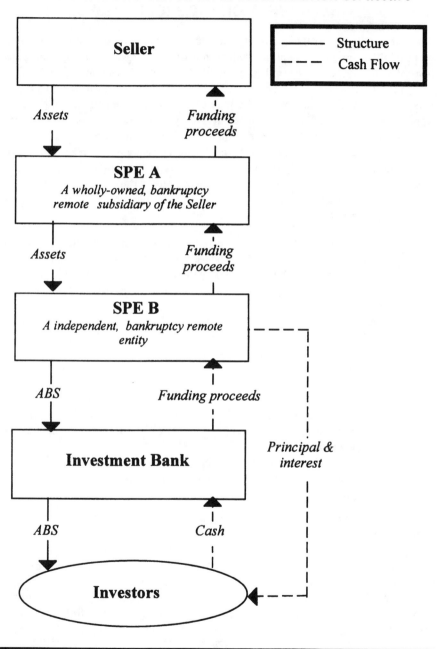

HOW CAN UNRATED ASSETS BE USED TO MAKE INVESTMENT GRADE SECURITIES?

Another nearly universal element of securitizations is the need for credit enhancement. Unlike the government guaranteed mortgages supporting many mortgage-backed securities, the collateral backing ABS and ABCP is subject to credit risk. Over the life of nearly every pool of securitizable assets — regardless of type — it is highly probable that some obligors will become delinquent and some lesser number will default. These defaults will likely result in the loss of collateral, potentially translating into payment delays or losses to investors.

The introduction of collateral performance risk creates uncertainty about the timing and amount of cash available to service the obligations of the SPE. Credit enhancement is used to offset this uncertainty and to limit investors' exposure to loss or payment delays. This enhancement may come from a variety of mechanisms, including:

- *Excess spread:* Collateral interest collections remaining after payment of investor coupons and fees can be used to offset non-performing assets.
- *Reserve fund:* Cash is deposited by the issuer, or excess spread is captured in a trust account. The funds are then used as needed to make principal and interest payments.
- *Overcollateralization:* The use of a larger pool of assets to support a smaller amount of securities. For example, $100 million of debt might be supported by $110 million in collateral.
- *Subordinated debt structure:* To access more funds than overcollateralization might allow, a SPE may issue more than one class of debt. In exchange for a higher return, subordinated debt holders will agree to absorb losses before senior debt holders. Using the previous example, $110 million of collateral might be able to support $100 million of AAA rated debt and $5 million of BBB rated debt.
- *Surety bond:* In exchange for a fee, an insurance company may be willing to issue a surety bond guaranteeing principal and interest payments to investors.[3]

The amount of enhancement required is usually determined on a transaction-specific basis by either the credit rating agency that rates the ABS or by the ABCP conduit funding the securitization. On rated transactions, the agency will evaluate a variety of the transaction's features including historical performance of the collateral and the experience of the seller and servicer, and determine a level of expected losses.[4] The amount of enhancement required is a multiple of this expected loss level. As a rule of thumb, a AAA or equivalent rating will require enhancement equal to at least five times the expected loss level, while a BBB or

---

[3] For a discussion of financial guarantees, see Chapter 6.
[4] The approach of one rating agency is discussed in Chapter 5.

equivalent rating might require no less than two times expected losses. Be fore-warned, however, that the credit sizing process is more sophisticated than just assigning a given loss multiple for a given rating. Required enhancement levels can vary substantially depending on the particular circumstances.

WHAT ARE THE TYPES OF SECURITIZATION AND HOW DO THEY DIFFER?

Although they share many of the elements outlined in the previous sections, *term* and *conduit transactions* operate and function differently. To some degree, they are substitutes for one another. Each has its own advantages and disadvantages which potential issuers need to be aware of these when evaluating options.

Term Securitizations

In a typical term transaction, a single originator sells a specified pool of receivables into a securitization that has funded the purchase by issuing asset-backed bonds. If the seller is a bank, the transaction may rely on a single SPE to issue the securities and buy the collateral while still achieving its desired tax and accounting treatment. But if the seller is subject to bankruptcy law, the two-tiered structure outlined in Exhibit 2 is often used.

The type of SPE used to issue the debt is usually a function of the type of asset being securitized. Amortizing assets, such as auto loans, rely predominantly on either a grantor or an owners trust as the funding SPE. Although a grantor trust is slightly simpler to use, and provides a cleaner answer to the issue of entity level taxation, it suffers from certain operational drawbacks. Grantor trusts are extremely limited in their ability to reinvest collected cash flows, and generally must pass all cash through to investors shortly after collection. Other important limitations include an inability to purchase new receivables after the initial sale (except for limited replacement of defective or ineligible receivables) and an inability to fund themselves using multiple senior interests. This last restriction means that grantor trust interests can only be divided by payment priority (i.e., senior and subordinate classes) and not by time. Given these restrictions, grantor trusts may be an unsuitable SPE choice for assets with either very long or very short lives. However, for many assets, like auto and equipment loans, the grantor trust remains well suited.

Another consideration about grantor trusts is that they issue ABS with long amortization periods, which are usually less attractive to investors. All else being equal, and assuming a positively sloped yield curve, investors are willing to pay less for a bond with a long amortization period than for a bond with a short amortization period.

In contrast to the grantor trust, an owners trust can issue bonds that can be tranched both by time and payment priority, normally resulting in lower funding cost. However, use of an owners trust can entail a slightly higher risk of entity level taxation. To help offset this risk, the SPE's organizational documentation often contains a provision that if it becomes subject to federal taxation, the entity will convert to a partnership. Similar to grantor trusts, partnerships typically pass income and expenses through to their partners.

Most amortizing collateral that is mortgage related is securitized using a business trust that elects REMIC status. REMIC status eliminates any issues with entity level taxes, and allows securities that are issued to be tranched both by average life and payment priority.

While these structures work well for assets with lives that span periods of years, they are ineffective for collateral with a life span of only weeks or months. In the term market, short-lived collateral like credit card or trade receivables is securitized using revolving trust structures. The life of a revolving structure is characterized by two phases. During the first, the revolving phase, receivable cash flow, net of interest and other expenses, is used to purchase new receivables. During the second phase, the payout or amortization period, net collected cash flow is used to retire debt. Because it can reinvest collected cash flows in new receivables, and subject to limitations can issue multiple series of debt, the master trust is the form of SPE most commonly used for revolving term securitizations.

Conduit Securitizations

An asset-backed conduit is a special purpose corporation that regularly buys interests in pools of financial assets from one or more sellers and funds these purchases by issuing commercial paper. Within the world of conduits are two major types: single-seller and multi-seller.

As its name suggests, a *single-seller conduit* buys interests from only one seller, and is usually a subsidiary of the conduit's sponsor. Single-seller conduits are self-administered programs that can be costly and administratively burdensome for the sponsor to operate. Still, single seller conduits can be an effective solution for sellers that generate, and can spread costs over, a high volume of receivables. For these reasons, single-seller conduits make up a fraction of the overall conduit market, and most often are operated by very large finance companies.

Multi-seller operations dominate the asset-backed conduit market. Again as the name suggests, multi-seller conduits invest in receivable interests and asset-backed securities issued by multiple sellers. Most multi-seller conduits are sponsored and administered by large commercial banks, and the sellers are, more often than not, bank customers.

Conduit securitizations share some similarities with term transactions. Conduits can securitize virtually all of the same kinds of assets that are found in the term market. They must also be structured to address the same bankruptcy, tax, and accounting issues as are faced by term securitizations. Like a term transaction, a two-step sale structure can be used to create an off-balance-sheet, bankruptcy remote transaction that functions as debt of the seller for tax purposes. Beyond these similarities, conduit securitizations differ from term transactions in numerous ways, particularly with respect to funding, methods of credit enhance-ment and the use of liquidity facilities.

One obvious difference from term transactions is that conduit transactions are funded using commercial paper. These commercial paper funding costs, plus con-duit program fees, are passed on to the seller. Since the price of commercial paper is always changing, funding costs change every time old ABCP matures and new ABCP is issued. From a seller's perspective, these changing costs are very similar to funding with floating-rate debt. Because this can create basis risk between the funding costs and the yield earned on the assets underlying the securitization, conduit operators often require that an interest rate hedge be put in place for the life of the transaction.

Credit enhancement is another area where conduits differ from term secu-ritizations. Unlike term transactions, multi-seller conduits rely on two layers of credit enhancement. The first layer, the seller level enhancement, is designed to off-set risks of asset delinquency and default as well as dilution of receivables that may arise from any claims that the underlying obligors may have against the seller. This seller level enhancement is intended only to insulate the conduit from the credit risks of a particular seller's assets, and cannot be used to cross-collateralize the assets of other sellers in a multi-seller program. Seller level enhancement usually takes the form of overcollateralization, subordination, or limited recourse to the seller. Rather than being sized to achieve a AAA rating like most term transactions, seller level enhancement is sized to meet the conduit's credit requirements, which are typically the equivalent of a lower investment grade rating, often A or AA. An actual transaction-specific credit rating is normally not required in a conduit trans-action, which can create significant cost savings for the issuer.[5]

Program level credit enhancement functions as a secondary layer of pro-tection for the conduit. It can be used to absorb credit losses from any seller in a multi-seller program, over and above the protection provided by the seller level enhancement. In addition, it can be relied on to bridge gaps between maturing com-mercial paper and receivables collections arising from a deterioration in asset qual-ity. The required amount of program enhancement will depend on historic portfolio performance, seller concentrations, program triggers, structure of the liquidity facilities, and the credit quality of the assets in the conduit. At the program level, enhancement is provided by a third party, usually in the form of a surety bond issued by an insurance company or a letter of credit issued by the sponsoring com-mercial bank. In either case, the rating of the enhancement provider should be at least as high as the desired rating of the commercial paper. The cost of program level enhancement is passed onto sellers as part of their program fees.

Liquidity protection is a central feature of conduit programs that is not typically found in term securitizations. Liquidity support facilities are designed to

---

[5] As a matter of practice, the rating agencies that provide the conduit with its credit ratings do review its transactions for compliance with eligibility and suitability criteria. Most of these reviews take place before a transaction closes. However, a few large, experienced administrators are allowed to have post-closing reviews. These post-closing reviews can significantly shorten the length of time needed to execute a trans-action.

cover any cash flow shortfall that would keep commercial paper investors from receiving timely repayment. These agreements are intended as protection against a market disruption that prevents the conduit from issuing new commercial paper or mismatches arising between maturing commercial paper and cash collected from the assets. However, liquidity support is not intended to serve as an additional source of credit enhancement, and will not usually cover timing disruptions arising from non-performing assets. Liquidity support normally takes the form of a committed line of credit issued from a commercial bank that typically already has a relationship with the seller. Liquidity providers typically must have a short-term credit rating equal to, or higher than, the conduit's own commercial paper rating. In general, the number of banks meeting these criteria and willing to provide liquidity is significant and the market can be competitive. However, conduit liquidity facilities usually cost the seller marginally more than it would pay for similar facilities based on it's corporate credit alone.

The cost of liquidity support varies by transaction and can be influenced by several factors, including the length of the agreement. Most agreements are 364 days long because banks are not required to hold risk-based capital against facilities maturing in less than one year. Because of this, banks will require a premium for facilities maturing beyond one year. Although it is common to match a multi-year conduit facility with a series of 364-day liquidity agreements, the mismatch introduces an element of cost uncertainty, sometimes referred to as *repricing risk*, over the life of the conduit agreement.

Several seller and asset related factors also influence liquidity cost. Among these are the seller's credit rating, the nature of the seller's business, and the quality, liquidity, and term of the assets. Liquidity providers focus on these issues in part because they influence the probability of their agreement being drawn upon. In addition, many liquidity support agreements, including those for most revolving conduit transactions, are structured with parallel purchase commitments. In the event the conduit cannot fund, these commitments can protect the interest of the seller by transferring ownership of the assets to the liquidity bank and requiring it to fund future purchases from the seller.

In general, more banks are willing to supply facilities to higher quality companies, and lower rated sellers tend to pay more than their higher rated counterparts for the same facility. Furthermore, because many large banks already have significant credit exposure to heavy borrowers like finance companies, these companies normally pay more for liquidity than similarly rated industrial firms. The assets securitized can also affect liquidity cost, because the provider may ultimately need to liquidate the assets to recoup its funds. All else being equal, the shorter lived or the more liquid the assets, the lower the liquidity costs will be.

Exhibit 3 illustrates the structure and cash flows of a typical off-balance-sheet conduit transaction. As with a term securitization, the seller transfers assets pursuant to a true sale to a wholly owned, bankruptcy remote subsidiary SPE, usually a special purpose corporation. Just as in Exhibit 2, this first transfer protects the assets for bankruptcy purposes, and sidesteps a taxable transfer. At this point, the structural similarities with a term transaction end. The SPE subsequently sells an undivided interest in the receivables and seller level credit enhancement to the conduit. In purchasing these interests, the conduit effectively fills the role of an ABS investor, which has funded its purchase through the sale of commercial paper. But unlike an investor in a term ABS transaction, the conduit can function in much the same way as a revolving line of credit, increasing and decreasing its investment to meet the operational and seasonal needs of the seller. This flexibility is one of the major operational advantages of a conduit financing.

The conduit structure also differs from a term transaction in that a trustee bank is only required if the seller SPE organized as a trust. In the absence of a trustee, the conduit administrator itself will assume responsibility for tasks like portfolio surveillance and reviewing the administration and collection of cash. Eliminating the trustee can be of significant benefit to the seller since it both lowers transaction costs and lessens the securitization's reporting burdens.

Exhibit 3: Structure of a Multi-Seller Conduit Transaction

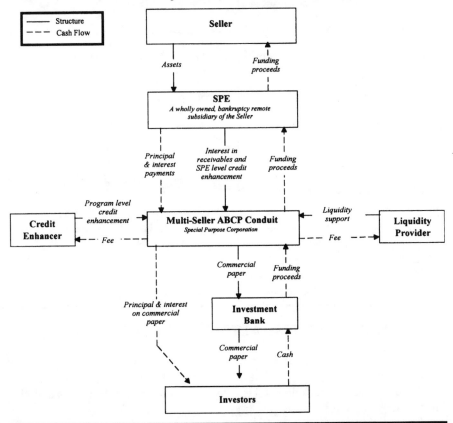

Exhibit 4: Securitization Options

	Multi-Seller Conduit	Private Placement	Public Issue
Typical Transaction Size	$25 million - $1 billion	$25 million - $150 million	$100 million +
Execution Time	4 - 6 weeks	8 - 12 weeks	12 - 16 weeks
First Time Set-up Costs	Low	Moderate	High
Accounting Treatment	Off-Balance-Sheet	Off-Balance-Sheet	Off-Balance-Sheet
Rating Requirements	May be optional	At least one rating required	At least two ratings preferred
Credit Enhancement	Overcollateralization, Cash Collateral Account, Letter of Credit, Surety Bond	Subordination, Overcollateralization, Cash Collateral Account, Letter of Credit, Surety Bond	Subordination, Overcollateralization, Cash Collateral Account, Letter of Credit, Surety Bond
Liquidity Agreements	Required	Not Required	Not Required
Funding Rate Basis	Spread off the CP or LIBOR Indices, basis can be swapped	Floating or Fixed, basis can be swapped	Floating or Fixed, basis can be swapped
Prepayment	Usually no penalty for payments or facility reductions made on payment dates (unless a interest rate hedge is involved)	Other than "clean-up calls," sponsor initiated prepayments are not allowed	Other than "clean-up calls," sponsor initiated prepayments are not allowed
Legal Structure	Collateral transferred via "true-sale" to bankruptcy remote, Special Purpose Corporation ("SPC")	Collateral transferred via "true-sale" to bankruptcy remote SPE	Collateral transferred via "true-sale" to bankruptcy remote SPE
Typical Documentation	- Transfer Agreement - Purchase Agreement - Liquidity Facility - Legal & Tax Opinions - Portfolio Audit	- Offering Memorandum - Sale Agreement - Pooling & Servicing - Agreement - Trust Indenture - Legal & Tax Opinions - Comfort Letter	- Prospectus & Registration Documents - Underwriting Agreement - Sale Agreement - Pooling & Servicing - Agreement - Trust Indenture - Legal & Tax Opinions - Comfort Letter
Financial Covenants	Sometimes - However, effects are minimal due to bankruptcy remote structure	Sometimes - However, effects are minimal due to bankruptcy remote structure	Very rarely
Operating Flexibility	High	Low	Low

Source: First Chicago Capital Markets, Inc.

HOW DO THESE ALTERNATIVES COMPARE?

Most companies considering a first-time securitization have three options available to them: a multi-seller conduit transaction, and a term transaction with either public or private execution. Exhibit 4 compares the three alternatives and highlights many of the differences.

Of the three options, the market for publicly registered term securitizations is the largest and probably the most widely understood. However, public securitizations can be the most expensive and time consuming of the choices, especially for a first-time issuer. Many factors contribute to the time and costs of public transactions, including the need for multiple credit ratings, the need for extensive legal documentation, and the registration of the transaction with the Securities and Exchange Commission. However, time and costs can fall after the initial transaction — new legal documents can be modeled from existing ones, SEC shelf registration can be used, and the rating agencies are already familiar with the seller and the collateral. Because the average issuance costs tend to fall as more transactions are executed, public securitizations are well suited to organizations that can generate enough collateral to support regular public ABS offerings.

Privately placed term transactions have most of the same features as public ABS, but can be less expensive and time consuming to execute. Often only a single credit rating is needed, and the transactions are exempt from SEC registration. Private execution can be an appropriate choice for sellers that want access to the term market but do not generate enough collateral to effectively access the public markets. Many growing firms and highly specialized finance companies fit this description. In some ways, the private market serves as an incubator for the public market. Many new issuers and asset types first debut in the private market, before graduating into the public market. But the private placement market is not limited to small or infrequent issuers. It is also a popular option for very complex transactions or for sellers desiring access to the term market with a minimum of disclosure or regulatory scrutiny. This latter reason helps explain why several commercial banks have chosen private execution for multi-billion dollar collateralized loan securitizations.

Of the three options, multi-seller conduits generally offer securitizers the greatest degree of flexibility for the lowest up-front costs. These costs are usually lower for several reasons, including the elimination of rating agency fees and the removal of the need for a prospectus, SEC registration, or underwriters' fees. In addition, the elimination of a trustee not only eliminates trustee expenses, but also obviates the need for a trust indenture, which in turn contributes to lower legal costs.

Depending on the particular conduit, securitizations between $25 million and $2 billion can be accommodated. For larger transactions, co-purchase arrangements which divide a seller's program between two or more conduits are increasingly common. Another advantage is that a typical conduit transaction can be executed in roughly half the time of a public transaction. Also, unlike term transactions, conduit deals can be resized with a minimum of effort and often without incremental cost, unless an interest rate swap or hedge needs to be adjusted. These features allow conduits to be more responsive to an originator's operating needs.

Even with all of their advantages, conduits can have some drawbacks from an issuer's perspective. One potential issue arises because some banks allocate the seller's credit exposure to conduit transactions, albeit not on a dollar for dollar basis. If bank credit exposure is a scarce resource for a seller, its management must decide if the conduit is the best use of that resource. By comparison, term ABS transactions very rarely have any effect on the availability of bank credit.

There may be other potential constraints with conduits. For instance, many conduits resist securitizing long-lived assets like mortgages in part because of the mismatch created by funding these assets with commercial paper, and the potential costs of hedging such a position. There is also some hesitancy because there is a risk the bank may have to take a long-dated asset on balance sheet at some future date. Recently however, a growing number of conduits have begun to invest in longer-lived assets. Fueling this change has been the development of advance arrangements that provide for the future securitization of these assets in the term market. These arrangements can mitigate the aforementioned risks, and allow the conduit to function as a securitized warehouse facility.

WHICH ALTERNATIVE IS BEST?

While all three options provide issuers access to the advantages of securitization, they are not perfect substitutes. Each has advantages and disadvantages which potential issuers need to evaluate in the context of their own needs and preferences. Potential issuers should also realize that term and conduit transactions are not mutually exclusive. Term and conduit transactions can and have been used together to craft securitization solutions tailored to meet issuers' specific needs.

Chapter 2

Structuring Efficient Asset-Backed Transactions

Len Blum
Managing Director
Head, Asset-Backed Banking Group
Prudential Securities Inc.

Chris DiAngelo
Partner
Dewey Ballantine

INTRODUCTION

Securitization allows an issuer to dissect the risks and rewards of investing in a pool of receivables. The risks can be allocated to those market participants that are in the best position to understand and absorb them and thus would do so at the lowest cost. The rewards can be allocated to those market participants who will pay the highest price (or will receive the lowest yield) for those rewards. Allocation of risk and reward, however, must be done in a way so that the transaction is acceptable given tax, legal, regulatory and accounting constraints. Furthermore, the structure must make sense within the originator's/issuer's financing plan. Optimally, the securitization should give the originator a form of sustainable, competitive advantage.

The investment banker's first goal is to understand the issuer's objectives. The securitization structure should address the issuer's needs; however, as discussed in this chapter, each of these needs must be analyzed with respect to the current market environment. Some issuer objectives may be absolute, whereas others may represent trade-offs and optimizations. Generally, consideration will be given to the amount of financing desired, the tenor of financing, cost considerations, cash flow requirements, accounting and tax objectives, as well as the originator's ability to retain risk and/or service the assets.

Once the investment banker has assessed the originator's goals and constraints, a deal team is assembled. Securitization teams tend to be fairly large and comprised of members that specialize in various facets of asset-backed finance. Examples of such sub-specialties are law, accounting, investment banking, securities modeling, origination practices, credit underwriting procedures, credit rating, and servicing practices.

The team's initial goal is to dissect the issuer's origination practices, pool of receivables, and servicing procedures. These factors are considered within the framework of the originator's operating position and environment.

Generally, once the deal team has analyzed a pool of receivables (and its servicing) and identified the risks and rewards that reasonably can be allocated out, the team often will bid the risk out to providers of credit enhancement. They also may decide to allocate certain risk to investors (for example, buyers of subordinated securities). The team will structure the securities with an eye towards specific investors who have expressed appetite for securities with characteristics that reasonably can be created from the pool. In many cases, the determination of structures will be based on estimates of what the parties will demand, because the actual marketing of the securities cannot take place until the structure is already set.

Information Flow and Pool Identification

The securitization process often provides feedback to the originator. As risks and rewards are analyzed, the specific costs of asset characteristics are made explicit. For example, if certain receivables are included in a pool, the cost may increase (either through more costly credit enhancement or higher security yields). In certain cases, a finance company, having gone through the securitization process, will make certain changes to its origination and/or servicing practices. In other cases, an originator may retain its origination practices and instead cull securitization pools, while selling or retaining those assets that cannot be securitized efficiently. The deal team often stands in the middle of this process and attempts to identify new risk and reward profiles of the asset pools and market participants as they arise. Not surprisingly, finance company treasurers/secondary marketing executives often have one foot on the loan origination side and the other in the asset-backed market.

Definition of Securitization

A securitization is a transaction in which a company effectively issues securities for which it is generally not corporately liable. The securities are backed by assets. Yet, securitizations can take on a broad variety of attributes that raise unique structuring issues.

COMPARISON TO OTHER FINANCING VEHICLES

Prior to discussing specific structural issues, it may be helpful to compare securitization with other corporate financing vehicles. This will provide a backdrop for many of the issues discussed in this chapter. Also, this will highlight the hybrid nature of securitization; securitization is neither a secured corporate financing nor a sale of assets. Rather, it incorporates certain aspects of both, while utilizing many of the well-accepted and fundamental legal, regulatory, tax, and accounting concepts commonly found in other financial transactions.

Whole-Loan Sales versus Securitizations

One market-driven feature that often distinguishes an asset-backed transaction from a whole-loan sale is that, while asset-backed transactions generally are done on a servicing-retained basis, whole loans usually are sold servicing-released because the purchaser (often itself an originator and servicer of such assets) will want to service the assets. This will, among other things, allow the purchaser to build portfolio scale economies, earn servicing revenue, cross-sell other products, and influence underlying borrower credit dynamics.

A second feature that distinguishes an asset-backed transaction from a whole-loan sale is the retention of credit and prepayment risk. In a whole loan sale, the seller often sells 100% of the credit risk and prepayment risk in the pool, yet it may make representations and warranties in connection with the sale and thus retain certain risks. Like a financing, the originator typically may retain credit risk. Yet, for the reasons described below, it is rare that the securitizing originator would transfer all of this risk; in most instances the issuing company economically retains at least the expected risk of loss on the asset pool, with the risk of certain disaster scenarios resulting in an unanticipated high level of credit losses being allocated either to a third-party credit enhancer, if any, and/or to investors.

A whole-loan sale may result in a premium execution, whereas an asset-backed sale usually does not involve an execution materially in excess of par (although premium execution may be achieved either directly or through the use of interest-only securities, as discussed later in this chapter). One reason that new issue securitizations, in most markets, generally trade at or near par is that premium securities create unique prepayment risk for the investor and typically are not found in the new issue market. Also, the issuer in an asset-backed transaction sometimes will retain a subordinate interest in the principal of the receivables pool or the issuer may make "excess servicing" (the difference between (1) the net pool coupon and (2) the bond coupon and other expenses) available for credit support (thereby precluding at least part of its use for backing the bond premium), or a combination thereof.[1] In other words, it frequently is not possible, for credit reasons, to exceed a par execution. Furthermore, even if it were possible for credit reasons to exceed par, the investor market is frequently not interested in premium execution or may demand a yield premium for such securities.

Securitizations are also distinguished from whole-loan sales by their cash-flow timing. In a securitization, flows from the assets often are reinvested in short-term investments, resulting in a payment lag feature in which investors receive their payments later than the dates on which these payments were received by the servicer. Payments from the loans also may be reinvested in additional loans of a similar type (this often occurs in credit card and trade receivables transactions), thereby causing the securities to have a longer average life than that of the

---

[1] Sometimes the availability of principal and interest (from a credit perspective) may be enhanced through the use of cash reserves or other features; however, there are economic implications (as discussed later) of such methods.

underlying pool. When certain asset pools, such as credit card portfolios, are sold (rather than securitized), both the accounts and the receivables that arise pursuant to such accounts are transferred (whereas a securitization would be backed only by the receivables arising pursuant to the accounts). Furthermore, securitization uses various forms of credit enhancement that protect the investor from losses on the loan pool (although certain forms of credit enhancement also can be found in whole-loan sales) and generally provides the investor with a more liquid holding.

Secured Financing versus Securitizations

Securitizations often are compared to secured financings. From a legal perspective, there is one primary feature that most distinguishes an asset-backed transaction from a receivables-secured financing. In an asset-backed transaction, although typically resulting in the issuance of notes or certificates (collectively referred to herein as "securities"), an issuing company is not *corporately* liable on its asset-backed securities. Investors primarily look only to the asset pool, together with any credit enhancement thereon.

The concept of asset-backed transactions resulting in the issuance of securities for which the issuing company is not itself generally liable is not immediately obvious. A helpful point of entry into the discussion of this peculiar issue is a familiar principle in corporate finance, that of defeased securities — outstanding corporate debt, that, after its issuance, is secured by the establishment of a Treasury escrow that results in the release of the original issuer from general corporate liability.

Defeased Debt versus Securitization

Corporate bond indentures often contain "defeasance" provisions. Such provisions allow a company that previously issued corporate debt to deliver to the bond trustee an escrow account; this account is pledged to repay the debt. The account typically must consist of Treasury bonds. It is structured such that the principal and interest payments on the Treasuries match, as closely as possible, the required principal and interest payments on the debt. A defeasance escrow typically is structured to minimize excess funds that may remain after payment of debt service. If any funds remain, they typically will flow back to the company. Defeasance is used when a company would like to redeem its debt, perhaps to relieve itself from restrictive covenants, but optional redemption is not currently available. A defeasance provision provides that, once the company has pledged the Treasury escrow, it will be released from paying the debt as a matter of corporate liability. Bondholders must thereafter look only to the escrow account to service the debt. Defeased debt, then, is somewhat unusual in that, post-defeasance, it looks like debt of the company, but it is debt for which the issuing company is not liable. Instead, the company's corporate liability has been replaced by the Treasury escrow.

Securitization achieves a similar goal for an issuer; namely, it provides for the issuance of securities by a company for which the company itself is not corporately liable. Instead of funding a Treasury escrow to support a pre-existing liability, a securitization establishes a receivables pool on day one. The company often will never be corporately liable on such debt. However, many of the economic risks may remain; the issuer, or an affiliate thereof, may continue to service the assets and the issuer (or an affiliate thereof) may have made representations and warranties about the loan pool and the transaction.

BANKRUPTCY FIREWALLS AND THE ISSUANCE VEHICLE

For most companies, the mitigation of corporate liability requires the establishment of a separate legal entity. Securitizations generally are structured such that this entity is the legal owner of the assets. As a result, the receivables pool would not legally be part of the company's property in the event of the company's bankruptcy. One exception to this rule is, to some extent, securitization for U.S. banks because federal banking laws are more favorable to creditors of insolvent banks than comparable provisions of the Bankruptcy Code are to creditors of Bankruptcy Code debtors. (Note that finance companies generally are subject to the Bankruptcy Code.) The only other common exceptions to the rule would be insurance companies that are subject neither to the Federal Bankruptcy Code nor to the federal banking laws but rather to state insolvency laws relating to insurance companies, and municipalities, that are subject to special provisions of the Federal Bankruptcy Code.

The type of legal entity that must be constructed to achieve the desired bankruptcy goals varies depending upon the structure of the transaction. The most commonly used legal entity in securitization is the common-law trust. This type of trust is generally referred to as a "business trust." It is quite different from testamentary or estate-planning trusts that individuals frequently establish. In most states, a business trust is an entity that conducts a business activity. Yet, like a corporation, it is a separate entity from its security holders. In this regard, a trust is similar to a corporation or a partnership.

There are several reasons why trusts are favored over corporations and partnerships as issuing vehicles. As a legal matter, a trust will tend to have fewer rules in terms of its establishment than will a corporation or a partnership. A corporation invariably requires articles, bylaws, officers, and directors. It also is required to issue at least one class of common equity. Similarly, a partnership requires partners, including at least one general partner, and a partnership agreement. Both corporations and partnerships generally are required to file certificates with the state in which they are formed. Although certain states, such as Delaware, have statutory provisions that allow the establishment of a statutory business trust that is more corporation-like than a common-law trust, in most cases this is not done unless some particular goal is sought. The common-law trust that generally is used does not require any particular formalities, except a declaration that a trust is being created.

The types of securities that a common-law trust can issue include various classes of debt and equity and generally are limited only by the imagination. The trust, being a separate legal entity, can also enter into other agreements, such as servicing agreements and indentures. Equity securities issued by a trust generally are structured as participation interests.

In a nutshell, the common-law trust is the most flexible issuing entity. There are fewer rules governing its establishment and operation. There is a lack of restrictions on the types of securities that a trust can issue. Furthermore, trusts can be used to achieve accounting sale treatment of the receivables pool (assuming other tests are met) by providing an easy vehicle for the issuance of participation interests. Yet, there may be, and frequently are, substantial federal income tax concerns, that, as a practical matter, limit the types of securities that a trust can issue.

Except for the federal income tax considerations discussed later, a trust generally is treated as a "pass-through entity." On the one hand, it is a separate legal entity for state and corporate law purposes; it can enter into contracts, issue securities and conduct ancillary activities. However, it is not an entity for federal and most state income tax purposes. Rather, it generally is a consolidated entity for tax purposes that will be consolidated into whatever entity owns the majority of the equity in the trust.

The establishment of a trust, however, is often not enough. Typically, in a securitization transaction, a *special purpose financing vehicle* (SPV) also is formed. An SPV is generally a corporation established (for bankruptcy purposes) as a separate legal entity from the seller/servicer. This is necessary because the seller/servicer usually ends up retaining at least the expected risk on the portfolio. This risk may be embedded in subordinate securities, subordinated excess servicing, or cash reserves. If the issuer itself were to hold this retained subordination, a bankruptcy risk may exist that, in the event of a bankruptcy of the originator/ seller/servicer (that is holding the retained subordination), a bankruptcy court could recharacterize the entire transaction as an issuance of secured debt of the originator/seller/servicer. This could leave the senior security holders with only a security interest rather than an ownership interest in the receivables pool. At the very least, this would create timing problems by subjecting the security holders to the risk of an automatic stay (commonly referred to as "stay risk").

Apart from stay risk, the bankruptcy law provides that secured creditors are entitled only to "adequate protection" rather than the exact protection that they may have thought they received at closing. Although specific outcomes are not fully known, the presumed risk is that the bankruptcy court could redirect cash flows or collateral to the detriment of the senior security holders, or force a sale of the collateral to repay the senior security holders and generate immediate cash for the bankruptcy estate. Having the subordinate interests that are issued by the trust held by an SPV mitigates these risks.[2]

---

[2] Yet even very conservative parties generally will allow at least some level of subordination to be held directly by the issuing seller servicer.

A legal opinion generally is given in connection with the securitization transaction to the effect that, in the event of a bankruptcy of the seller/servicer, counsel issuing the opinion believes that the SPV and the seller/servicer's estates would not be consolidated as a single entity for bankruptcy purposes. The SPV, although often set up as an affiliate of the seller/servicer, is established pursuant to a formula that ensures its separateness in a bankruptcy. In other words, it should be treated as a third-party entity vis-à-vis the seller/servicer, even though it may be a wholly-owned subsidiary.

In a typical SPV structure, the seller/servicer legally will sell the assets to the SPV. The SPV, in turn, will sell the assets to the trust. The trust then issues participation interests in the asset pool to investors, with the subordinate interest being retained by the SPV. For federal tax considerations, the sale from the originator to the SPV is meaningless because the SPV will be consolidated as part of the parent company's tax financial statements; under GAAP, as required by SFAS 125, the transfer to an SPV which is a "qualifying" SPV under SFAS results in sale treatment, since (unlike as for tax), the qualifying SPV is a "deconsolidated" entity which is not part of the parent's consolidated financial statements.

The sale by the SPV to the trust, in and of itself, does not trigger an event for tax reporting. However, the sale of the participation interests to investors (i.e., a sale outside of the affiliated group of originator-SPV-trust) may effect a tax event (that may or may not receive parallel treatment depending on the transaction's structure). This is contrasted with the bankruptcy and GAAP analysis, in that the sale from the company to the SPV is treated as a sale for Federal Bankruptcy Law and GAAP purposes. One result of using the SPV structure is the isolation of the asset pool from the reach of the originator's general creditors or other secured creditors by transferring the pool, as a legal matter, to the SPV. The sale from the SPV to the trust, although potentially also resulting in a sale for bankruptcy purposes, may be less important to the bankruptcy analysis, where the key goal is to remove the asset pool from the legal property of the company.

Not all asset-backed transactions use trusts. The most frequent alternative to the establishment of a trust is simply the issuance of debt from an SPV.

Securitizations should not only be "bankruptcy remote," but also be "bankruptcy proof." As discussed, bankruptcy remoteness is achieved in two principal ways. First, the assets are legally sold to the SPV. Second, the SPV is established and operated in a manner that ensures it could not be consolidated with the company in the event of the company's bankruptcy. However, additional protection is usually required as well. The SPV should be constructed so that it cannot engage in activities that would expose it to undue risk on its own (as distinguished from risks arising through consolidation). Among other things, an SPV generally is restricted from incurring recourse debt and engaging in an operating business (such as originating or servicing loans).

In summary, the principal elements on the bankruptcy checklist are as follows:

- Has a sale of the assets occurred to legally remove them as property of the company and make them property of the SPV?
- Could the SPV be consolidated with the company in the event of the company's bankruptcy?
- Is the SPV constructed so as to mitigate the risk that it could go into its own bankruptcy?

One final bankruptcy issue relates to the bankruptcy opinion (often called a "true sale" opinion) that is given by legal counsel in an asset-backed transaction. Bankruptcy courts refer to themselves as "courts of equity" rather than "courts of law." This means that the courts have significant discretion to use their judgement within the guidelines of the Federal Bankruptcy Laws. As a result, structuring bankruptcy-proof transactions is more of an art than a science. The opinions that are given by even the most competent counsel tend to be "reasoned" opinions. They reflect both sides of the argument and often only give their conclusions in a tenuous manner.

Some people incorrectly believe that the true sale opinion is the last word on the issue and that the opinion itself makes the transaction isolated from a bankruptcy point of view. This is not true. Legal opinions from a private law firm, unlike court opinions rendered by a judge, do not conclusively establish a result. Opinions, however, do let the rest of the deal team know that a presumably competent lawyer has studied the bankruptcy implications of the transaction and has concluded that, on balance, the transaction should achieve the desired bankruptcy result. The opinion also transfers some liability to the law firm (and its insurance carrier) to the extent that the opinion is wrong. As a practical matter, however, given the reasoned nature of most of these opinions, the chances of liability are slim.

UNDERLYING CONSIDERATIONS OF FINANCING VERSUS SALE FOR GAAP AND TAX

An asset-backed transaction can be structured, within certain limits, for GAAP and tax reporting, either as a financing or as a sale. What many issuers want to accomplish when they first hear about asset-backed finance is to try to achieve the best of both worlds, namely, an accounting sale and a tax financing.

An accounting sale transforms the receivables into cash without creating a related liability (basically, cash is debited and receivables are credited). Depending on the use of proceeds, such a transaction can enhance leverage ratios and improve capital velocity. Conversely, if the transaction is structured as a GAAP financing, the assets remain on the balance sheet, the cash account is debited, and a corresponding liability is credited. (The characteristics of accounting sales and financings are covered in greater detail in Chapter 7.) For "above-water" assets (generally those assets with coupons approximately at current market rates) that have relatively long average lives (e.g., mortgages), GAAP sale treatment can trigger a material gain (as a percentage of the pool), that can enhance earnings in the period of sale.

Tax sales and financings often result in the same expected aggregate tax liability over the life of the transaction. However, a sale can trigger a taxable gain at the time of the transaction, thereby accelerating taxes that otherwise would be due during the asset's life. Due to cash flow and time value of money considerations, most originators would rather defer this tax liability over the life of the pool.

Although sometimes a worthwhile goal, as a practical matter, financing-for-tax treatment is often inefficient for several asset classes (for example, home-equity and manufactured-housing loans). The inefficiencies required to accomplish this treatment frequently outweigh the benefits from having the result. (As discussed below, however, such treatment is readily available for certain asset classes, such as credit card accounts and trade receivables). In many instances, the most economically efficient structure would result in a sale transaction for tax purposes. To demonstrate this, it is useful to provide an overview of one of the most basic, as well as one of the most difficult concepts, in the general area of tax law: the difference between debt and equity.

Tax Debt and Equity

For tax purposes, securities are naturally equity in form. If a company issues only a single class of securities, those securities would be treated as an ownership interest (equity); the security holders would be entitled to receive all the revenues generated by the entity after the payment of expenses. To distinguish debt from equity, the purported debt needs to be given some characteristics and/or form to distinguish it from the equity. This is normally not a problem with an operating company. An operating company's debt, in addition to its contractual payment requirements, typically has a precise form, for example, a set interest rate, a payment frequency, a maturity date, and other characteristics that are taken for granted when an operating company issues debt. Its contractual payment is not directly correlated to the cash flows from the company's operations.

The issue becomes more complex, however, in a securitization because the issuing entity is not an operating company; instead, it only holds financial assets in the form of a receivables pool. The receivables in a pool are typically themselves debt instruments. They typically pay monthly pursuant to their debt-service schedules. Asset-backed securities also are often monthly pay. Because of this high correlation between debt service and revenues, it is often difficult to conclude that any securities issued in such an arrangement, whether styled as debt or as equity, are anything other than equity, especially when they account for a vast majority of a trust's revenues. This is different from the operating company, where revenues are not based on a schedule. Corporate debt, furthermore, is not typically monthly pay, but may rather be semi-annual pay, yet the company may receive revenues on a daily basis. Therefore, it is unlikely that corporate debt would be seen as constituting an ownership interest in the revenues of an operating company, at least in part, because the debt service requirements on the corporate debt are so clearly distinct from the revenues of the company.

In the United States, as distinguished from certain European countries, the economic substance of a transaction, rather than its form, governs (or at least greatly influences) the tax characterization. In other words, the form of a security does not dictate its classification. For example, if a company were to (1) transfer $100 million dollars in receivables that bear interest at 8% to a trust, (2) issue notes with a face amount of $100 million dollars that bear interest at 7.9%, and (3) construct the debt service schedule on the notes such that principal was payable on the notes only when the trust itself received principal payments on the underlying receivables, it would be difficult to conclude that the company had done anything other than sell a receivables pool. The "debt" that purports to be "secured" by the pool looks just like the pool itself. Characterizing this transaction as an issuance of debt typically would not fly as a matter of tax law.[3]

Of course, form may help in the determination of whether a security is debt or equity. To make a security "look like debt," it is helpful to call it debt (for example, to refer to the security as "notes" or "bonds" rather than "certificates").

For tax purposes, besides simply calling securities debt, it is usually necessary to distinguish the debt from some equity component of the issuing entity. When a trust issues debt it will typically issue some other type of security as a residual interest that may be represented by certificates. Also, as a general matter, the less debt that a company is trying to raise against a given pool of collateral, the easier it is to conclude that the securities will be treated as debt. In general, if the originator retains a larger interest, it is easier to conclude that the assets have not been sold for tax purposes because the risk of ownership of the assets remains with the issuer.

Securities look more like debt when an issuer "breaks the chain" between its revenues and its debt service. In the true corporate context, this is usually the case when an issuer's revenues are not tied to any fixed schedule, but its debt is. In asset-backed transactions, the revenues are tied to a fixed schedule. Unless the debt is consciously disengaged from this schedule, it may resemble equity.

Often, to create tax debt, payment features are altered. For example, the interest rate on the debt (for example, fixed rate) can be set independent of the interest rate on the receivables pool (for example, floating rate), the payment frequency of the debt (for example, semiannual pay or quarterly pay) can differ from that of the receivables pool (for example, monthly pay), or the debt can have a maturity date that does not correspond with that of the receivables. Yet such measures often are economically inefficient. For example, disengaging the interest rates of the

---

[3] In contrast, the form of a transaction can dictate (or influence) its treatment under GAAP. Under SFAS 77 and under SFAS 125, effective after December 31, 1996, for a transfer of receivables to be treated as a sale, it must purport to be one. This would preclude sale treatment for asset-backed transactions that issue securities in the form of "notes" or "bonds."

receivables and the debt not only introduces risk to the residual holder, but also may introduce negative marketing characteristics. For example, if fixed-rate receivables were to back an available-funds floater, investors may be concerned with the cap if the weighted-average coupon of the pool was too low (obviously, this also may create credit enhancement implications). Creating quarterly or semiannual-pay securities from monthly-pay assets creates reinvestment risk during the period between receipt on the assets and payment on the securities. Also, these funds generally must be invested in low-yield, short-term instruments. Mismatching maturity dates may create the need for costly maturity guarantees or reinvestment accounts.

Credit Card Securitizations

As mentioned, certain types of collateral lend themselves more easily to the creation of debt. Revolving accounts (for example, credit card accounts and commercial trade receivables accounts) are prime examples. Since the medium-term asset-backed debt is closed-end (i.e., not revolving), but is backed by short-term receivables arising pursuant to accounts, there is a significant mismatch between the underlying receivables (at any point in time) and the outstanding debt. Given the fact that in a credit card securitization the receivables pool itself fluctuates up and down, and revolves, credit card deals typically are treated as the issuance of debt by the credit card issuer for tax purposes. For GAAP accounting purposes, however, these transfers of assets are treated as sales if they meet the requirements of SFAS 125. Other than for estimable credit losses, there is no recourse to the issuer (for example, the issuer does not guarantee the market value of the pool). Call options generally are de minimus (5% to 10%).

Mortgage Securitization

It is difficult to achieve tax debt treatment for closed-end mortgages for a number of reasons. First, unlike credit card accounts, mortgages do not revolve and are long-term. Second, because of their high credit quality, most mortgages may be monetized at or near par. As noted above, the higher the advance rate, the more difficult it is to conclude that the issuer has issued debt backed by the pool. Also, "chain-breaking" features tend to introduce economic inefficiencies. For example, a company could issue semi-annual- or quarterly-pay securities backed by a pool of monthly-pay mortgage loans; however, this would potentially expose the issuing company to negative arbitrage. The reinvestment rate on the monthly receipts may not cover the interest rate on the asset-backed debt since the monthly receipts would generally be reinvested in "cash-equivalent" investments. A company may issue floating-rate securities backed by fixed-rate mortgages (or vice versa); however, this introduces interest-rate risk and available funds concerns. Of course, a company may issue securities for materially less than the par amount of the mortgages; however, for most issuers, this would not be desirable.

In addition, for mortgages there are a series of interlocking federal tax requirements, primarily the real estate mortgage investment conduit (REMIC) rules and the taxable mortgage pool (TMP) rules. The REMIC rules were created by the Tax Reform Act of 1986. These rules provide that a REMIC can issue multiple classes of "regular interests" (similar to debt), but only one "residual interest" (similar to equity). They essentially create a safe harbor for mortgage-backed securities by alleviating the risk of double taxation, since REMICs are not taxed at the entity level. The residual holder generally is taxed in a similar manner to a partner in a partnership.

Largely due to REMIC, the asset-backed community has devised multi-class, mortgage-backed structures that are almost 100% efficient. A study of non-conforming mortgage deals (i.e., deals not involving Fannie Mae, Freddie Mac, or Ginnie Mae) from 1990 to 1995 shows an evolution beginning with retained subordination transactions, in which the issuing company received less than a 100% advance rate, and often had payment mismatches. Transactions then evolved to "spread account deals" that involved setting up a reserve account and funding it from excess servicing. From there, the current and widely accepted Prudential Accelerated Credit Enhancement (PACE) structure evolved, in which excess servicing is used to accelerate the amortization of the asset-backed securities relative to the amortization of the underlying mortgage loans.[4] As a result, this creates a subordinate security (that may be a residual) over time. Spread account and PACE structures often give the issuer an advance rate of par or near par at the time of issuance.

The REMIC rules are flexible and appreciated by the asset-backed community. Yet, the REMIC rules also require that the issuing company treat the transaction as a tax sale. For GAAP purposes, depending on the specifics of a transaction, a REMIC can be treated as either a sale or a financing.[5] The taxable mortgage pool rules further complicate the issue by providing that any multi-class transaction that can be done as a REMIC, namely, just about any multi-class transaction involving mortgage loans, must be done as a REMIC (except pro-rata pay classes that may differ in payment priority). This means that it is difficult to do an asset-backed transaction with a pool of mortgage loans other than as a transaction that achieves a tax sale. One of the sinister beauties of the interlocking federal tax statutes regarding the issuance of mortgage-backed securities is that even a REMIC transaction that is styled as debt is unlikely to achieve debt treatment for federal income tax purposes for the issuer.

Although most REMICs are accounted for as GAAP sales, it is not difficult to achieve non-parallel, GAAP-financing treatment. This can be done, for

---

[4] Two of the advantages of the overcollateralization structure are: (1) the elimination of the negative arbitrage that results from the cash reserve account; and (2) the shortening of the weighted-average life of the asset-backed securities, thereby bringing them "down the yield curve" and creating a lower cost of funding in an ascending yield curve environment.

[5] This fact should not be confused with the further fact that REMIC also provides that "regular interests" issued by the REMIC will be treated as debt in the hands of the security holders as a matter of the REMIC law. This aspect of the REMIC treatment is also non-parallel treatment, but deals with looking at a REMIC transaction from both the issuing company's point of view (sale) and from the security holder's point of view (debt).

example, by introducing a material call (or put) option which would overcome sale treatment under SFAS 125. A structure that is sometimes used in higher interest-rate environments is the "underwater" REMIC. In such a transaction, assets worth less than their amortized tax basis are securitized, thereby triggering a tax loss. Yet the introduction of a material call (or put) agreement under SFAS 125 ensures that an accounting loss will not be accelerated because for GAAP purposes, the assets have not been sold.

Recent legislation has created a new tax vehicle, the financial asset securitization investment trust (FASIT), which extends REMIC benefits to other asset classes such as auto loans and credit card receivables, although under a separate statutory authorization from REMIC. The FASIT structure has not been widely used.

Since non-conforming mortgage deals are thus currently structured as REMICs to achieve almost 100% efficiency, any non-REMIC, debt-for-tax, sale-for-GAAP structure would have to be overpoweringly useful in its tax-deferral achievements to beat this almost perfect economic efficiency. Any "chain-breaking" necessary to achieve debt-for-tax treatment potentially would introduce substantial economic inefficiencies and make the transaction impractical, absent other compelling objectives, such as a need to maximize after-tax proceeds in the short term, even though the long-term cost implications would be suboptimal.

Other Asset Securitization

Between trade receivables and credit cards, on one side of the spectrum, and mortgage loans, on the other, fall many other asset classes, such as auto loans and equipment leases. Although these asset types generally do not revolve as credit card accounts do, they typically do not lend themselves to the extreme efficiency that residential mortgages do. For example, for credit and other reasons, it is usually not possible to achieve a a par or near par advance rate. Since the advance rate is lower for these asset classes, fewer efficiencies need to be created to construct a debt-for-tax, sale-for-GAAP structure.

Although auto loans themselves do not revolve, one can make the pool artificially revolve by adding receivables over time to the initial pool. The practice has thus developed to achieve non-parallel treatment in the form of debt-for-tax, sale-for-GAAP with auto loans and similar types of assets to have a revolving structure such that, for a certain period, principal amortization on the asset pool, instead of being paid through as a payment in principal to the security holders, is used to purchase more assets, thus making the securities "interest-only" during the revolving period (an obvious break in the chain from the underlying receivables that themselves amortize every month). This revolving feature, together with a less-than-100% advance rate and a few other miscellaneous bells and whistles, has been known to achieve debt-for-tax, sale-for-GAAP treatment.

In summary, it is possible to achieve sale-for-GAAP/financing-for-tax treatment for any type of asset pool. The issue rather is the trade off between the benefits of the tax deferral on the one hand versus the cost of adding debt-like features on the other. Transactions have become more economically efficient (aside from tax considerations) and credit-related efficiencies have made transactions more difficult to do as tax financings. Furthermore, not all of the costs of adopting a debt-for-tax structure may be known at the time of the transaction. For example, the cost of a semi-annual pay structure on the securities to "break the chain" from a monthly-pay receivables pool will be largely driven by reinvestment rates during the transaction. Consequently, debt-for-tax, sale-for-GAAP remains, at least outside of credit card, trade receivables, and certain other transactions, an increasingly elusive goal.

EFFICIENT ALLOCATION OF RISK — CREDIT RISK

The market for asset-backed securities is in large part a "triple A" market. In other words, asset-backed securities generally are rated in the highest rating category by at least one (and often two, but sometimes more) of the nationally recognized statistical rating agencies (Moody's, Standard & Poor's, Fitch Investors Service, and Duff & Phelps). Note, however, that asset-backed securities also are issued at the AA, A, or BBB levels and, once in a while, even in noninvestment grade or unrated designations. To enable a pool of receivables to back high-grade, fixed-income securities generally requires credit enhancement.

External Enhancement

There are two major types of credit enhancement: external and internal. External enhancement can take the form of an insurance policy issued by a financial guarantee insurance company, a letter of credit issued by a bank, a corporate guarantee, or a reserve account funded by a third party. These credit enhancements rely on a party other than the asset pool itself to provide protection to security holders.

The simplest form of external credit enhancement is an insurance policy that covers 100% of the principal and interest on the asset-backed securities (other forms of credit enhancement often cover less than 100%). This type of insurance is issued by monoline insurance companies, which themselves have a AAA-rated claims-paying ability.

Internal Enhancement

Internal credit enhancement takes a variety of forms, although the most prevalent are senior/subordinated ("overcollateralization") structures, internally funded reserve accounts, and PACE structures. In a relatively simple senior/subordinated structure, the advance rate of issuance of the receivables pool, for example, is 90%. The 10% subordinated interest could be retained by an SPV affiliate of the company. Losses, in effect, would be charged against the subordinate security before the senior security holders would begin to suffer losses.[6] Note that more than one level of subordination can be utilized in a single transaction. For example, a transaction can be structured where the most subordinated interest (which may be a reserve fund or a subordinated interest) is retained by an SPV and mezzanine tranches are sold to investors. In a reserve account structure, the excess servicing funds an account pursuant to a formula. Available monies from the reserve account are used to cover losses as they occur during the life of the transaction.

Time tranching, which is discussed in more detail below, can be an important tool in structuring subordinated securities. Subordinated securities can be either structured as *pro-rata* or *sequential pay*. (Such tranching has important tax implications.) In a typical pro-rata pay structure consisting of one senior and one subordinate security, both securities will receive principal during the life of the transaction. Assuming no losses are allocated to the subordinate security, the level of subordination (the percentage interest that the subordinated security bears to the pool as a whole) will remain constant. In a sequential-pay structure, the subordinate security may only receive principal once the senior security has been paid in full.[7] In such a transaction, the level of subordination increases over time, which may allow for a lower level of initial subordination and/or may make the senior securities more marketable (of course, with a potential corresponding decrease in the marketability of the subordinated interest). Additionally, senior security holders may find such a structure more desirable if losses on the pool are expected to be relatively back-loaded. Consideration should be given to static loss curves when engineering such structures.

Combining External and Internal Enhancement

Even transactions that have external credit support such as an insurance policy will also have internal enhancement. This is most obvious again in the case of monoline insurance, where the monoline insurers typically will not insure the senior security unless the senior security is rated at an investment-grade level independent of the insurance policy. Although monolines have the power to insure transactions that have an internal rating of less than BBB, their economics of doing so diminish rapidly because, at least in part, the insurers themselves are subject to regulation in the form of the analysis of their capital adequacy by the rating agencies.

Sometimes mezzanine and senior classes within the same transaction are both afforded the enhancement of an insurance policy. This is often referred to as a "super-senior" structure. In such a transaction, the pool typically would be enhanced to at least a BBB level. This could be achieved through the use of a reserve account, a retained subordinated interest, PACE structuring, or some other method. The resulting investment-grade interest is then further credit tranched,

---

[6] Yet, if losses (and/or anticipated losses) are higher than originally anticipated (even when the senior interest is not being allocated such losses), the market value and/or the credit rating of such securities may deteriorate due to the reduced level of actual and/or expected protection afforded by the subordinate interest.

[7] Other variations are possible. For example, the subordinate security could receive principal once certain targets or formulas are met.

with a mezzanine interest that enhances the senior interest to, say, a AA or AAA level. Both the mezzanine interest and the senior interest are then guaranteed by a monoline. The resulting mezzanine and senior bonds would both achieve AAA ratings. The mezzanine bond would achieve this level because of the guarantee, but the senior bond would enjoy this level of support from both the enhancement afforded by the subordinated and mezzanine classes, as well as the guarantee. This structure has sometimes been used when investors in the senior securities require "belt and suspenders" enhancement or are concerned about saturation in their portfolio (or the market in general) for a particular monoline's credit.

Providers of external credit enhancement generally do not expect to themselves suffer any losses as a result of the performance of the receivables pool. This distinguishes, for example, a monoline insurer from a company that sells life insurance. The life insurer expects to have claims under its policies while the monoline would be surprised if a loss was charged against one of its transactions.

Conceptually, the monolines provide catastrophic risk coverage. In addition, they perform their own due diligence prior to closing and conduct an important surveillance function during the life of the transaction. They also may be more likely than a trustee (or other transaction participants) to step in and take action if there are material servicing problems. They also potentially make investor credit risk easier to analyze, which can add value particularly to a transaction involving a new issuer and/or new asset class.

Credit Enhancement Decisions

Credit enhancement decisions generally are made based on relative costs. The investment banker will typically consider various forms of credit enhancement and present them to the issuer. Generally, there are two major considerations: allocations to third parties and retained risk by the originator.

If the banker has an understanding of the costs of assuming risk by various parties, the decision of how to allocate third-party risk is fairly straightforward. In a very simple example, once a pool is internally enhanced to the BBB level, either BBB securities could be sold or a monoline could guarantee the securities to a AAA level. The decision between these two alternatives will be based, along with other qualitative and economic factors, on the spread differential between wrapped, AAA, senior securities and unwrapped, senior BBB securities on the one hand, and the premiums charged by monolines on the other.

These alternatives also could be compared to a mezzanine structure, where the risk could be further tranched into multiple securities, for example, AA, A, and BBB bonds. In such a structure, however, one must also consider deal size (a small pool would only allow creation of small tranches, which may trade poorly due to liquidity or "hassle factor" considerations) and loss severity (a credit loss to a smaller security will have a relatively larger impact). When analyzing such a structure, however, the banker must consider the effect of the structure on all of the sold bonds. For example, if mezzanine subordination is used versus a surety wrap, investors may view the risks of the AAA senior bonds differently. On the one hand, they neither would carry surety event risk (the risk of a negative credit deterioration of the surety) nor expose the investor to saturation of any given insurer. Yet they would have a lower percentage of enhancement and may have less ongoing surveillance, as well as be more difficult to analyze.

Qualitative issues also should be considered. For example, non-investment grade or unrated servicers potentially could not be used in a senior/subordinated structure when highly rated securities are to be issued (unless, of course, a creditworthy master servicer was retained or other transactional features, such as triggers — which are often found in credit card deals — are used). Also, some third-party insurers may have sufficient familiarity with the issuer or asset class to facilitate the credit analysis process. Due to competition or service quality considerations, some parties also may offer quicker turn-around and greater flexibility.

The amount of risk retained by the originator is often, at least in part, dictated by its cost and availability of capital. As a general rule, as the issuer's capital cost increases (or availability decreases), the more desirable it is for the issuer to sell a larger percentage of the pool. For example, an originator could either retain a large subordinate security and sell AAA bonds or retain a small subordinate security and sell BBB bonds. In the first instance, the issuer's savings on the sold securities (based on the fact that the issuer is retaining more risk and passing along less risk to investors) potentially could be outweighed by the cost of carrying the larger subordinate interest.

Furthermore, retaining the larger subordinate interest may negatively impact the issuer's ability to grow (by decreasing the velocity of its capital), accounting ratios (by decreasing liquidity and reducing funds that potentially could be used to reduce leverage) and earnings in the period of sale (by selling less of the asset and thereby recognizing less of a gain in such period). Conversely, the issuer may be in the best position to understand the risks of the assets and control or at least influence them through proper servicing. In this case, even for a capital-constrained entity, it may be preferable for the issuer to retain larger amounts of risk. In some cases, such as the securitization of risky, servicing-intensive assets, investors take additional comfort when the issuer has retained significant credit risk and "servicing upside."

Determining Credit Enhancement Levels

Credit enhancement levels for asset-backed securities are typically based on two primary factors. The first factor is the asset pool itself — the creditworthiness of the borrowers on the underlying receivables, the diversity of the pool, and to what extent the receivables themselves are secured. The second factor is servicing.

As may be expected, when the credit quality of the underlying asset pool is low, servicing practices are more important. A portfolio of weaker receivables would presumably require more work to extract a given level of payments than would a higher quality pool. In one extreme example, a Treasury bond portfolio requires no servicing other than maintaining a filing cabinet in which to keep payment records. Contrast this to many of the so called "sub-prime" markets in which lenders make loans to borrowers who would be unable to obtain credit from more traditional sources. Such loans often are serviced in a more rigorous fashion.

Enhancement requirements often are set at high multiples of historic performance. To ensure high credit quality of structured securities, which is reflected by high credit ratings, transactions are structured to withstand extreme stress-case scenarios. Also, enhancement levels reflect servicing risk and the risk that servicing could deteriorate during the life of the transaction. Also note that as a particular asset type becomes more familiar to market participants, credit enhancement requirements tend to decline. Still, there often are things that a transaction team can do to reduce required enhancement. A detailed discussion of these is beyond the scope of this chapter; however, some of the more common concepts are as follows:

- The deal team should ensure that the risks of the pool are adequately understood by enhancers, investors and the rating agencies. This should include static and dynamic pool analysis gathered over a significant period, and an analysis of underwriting, servicing, and collection practices. All risks should be adequately disclosed. Not only is this an essential general practice, but also it may enhance marketability. As a general rule, astute investors prefer to assume the risks they comprehend rather than to assume potentially lower risks that they do not clearly understand.

- The originator should analyze how its origination and servicing practices affect its securitization program. In certain circumstances, it may pay for the servicer to upgrade its operations and/or tighten its underwriting criteria. Sometimes, transaction participants, such as a credit enhancer, will require that a master servicer be retained. Also, profitable high risk loans potentially can be culled from the pool and retained or sold in the whole-loan market.

- Structural triggers should be analyzed. These triggers are commonly found in revolving structures. Triggers can require the build up of additional enhancement or the early amortization of securities in the event of a credit deterioration. Generally, the tighter the triggers, the lower the required credit enhancement. Yet tight triggers present greater cash flow, interest-rate, and availability risk to the issuer.

- Allocating specific risks to third parties should be considered. For example, residual value insurance can increase advance rates in operating lease transactions.

- Cross collateralization among transactions or among specific pools within a transaction should be considered. Sometimes, third parties will reduce required credit enhancement if subordinate instruments from a series of transactions are allowed to be cross collateralized. Yet this can decrease the issuer's flexibility in later financing or selling such subordinated interests.

TARGETING SPECIFIC INVESTORS

Besides the risk of credit loss, pools of receivables may contain prepayment risk or have average lives, principal windows and maturities that are relatively less attractive to investors. Time and prepayment tranching can be used to address these concerns and optimize execution.

Investment bankers constantly monitor the secondary market. From day to day, they are aware of specific investor preferences. When relatively strong investor demand exists in a particular sector (or weak demand exists in another), they can use that information to structure a transaction targeted to the preferences of the market.

Time Tranching

Tranching often involves the issuance of several series of securities against a single pool of receivables in a sequential-pay structure. Generally, all of the series receive interest during their lives (although this does not have to be the case); however, the first series receives all of the principal from the underlying pool until it is paid in full, after which the second series begins to receive principal. This process is repeated with subsequent classes until all of the securities are retired. In this way, a pool of receivables can be carved into a number of securities that may feed the appetites of particular investors or classes of investors.

As a mechanical matter, the expected characteristics of a particular time-tranched security generally will depend on the underlying pool and the principal balance of the security itself, as well as the principal balances of the other securities issued. To illustrate, imagine a pool of receivables backing two time-tranched (fast-pay/slow-pay structure) securities. As the principal balance of the fast-pay security is increased, its expected maturity, expected average life and expected principal window also will increase. At the same time, the maturity of the slow-pay security will remain unchanged (its final payment will not be affected), yet its expected average life will increase (because its earlier cash flows have been allocated to the fast-pay security), and its expected principal window will shorten (because it will receive principal over a shorter period of time). This concept can be applied to a larger number of tranches with more complex, yet similar, results.

In some market environments, the more time-tranched securities that can be created (up to a limit, of course), the lower the issuer's all-in cost will be. This may allow the issuer to target specific investor demands, take advantage of the shape and slope of the yield curve and shorten principal windows. Please note that certain asset types lend themselves more to tranching than do others. Also, the creation of a large number of tranches often requires a large asset pool because a small asset pool may result in very small tranched securities, which generally would be illiquid and demand a yield premium. Appropriate time tranching also allows for the reduction of specific tranche sizes, thereby alleviating concerns of sector saturation.

Time tranching also allows pricing of specific securities at premiums and discounts. For example, in a given transaction and market environment, buyers of longer tranches may demand pricing at a discount from par (hence a lower coupon), whereas buyers of shorter tranches may accept premium pricing (hence a higher coupon).

Coupon and Volatility Tranching

More elaborate tranching mechanics besides the relatively simple "sequential pay" structure also have been devised; however, they have been slower to catch on in the asset-backed markets than in the mortgage-backed markets. Perhaps this is partially because asset-backed collateral presents less prepayment risk; therefore, there is less need to allocate this risk to various classes of investors. One fairly common tranche in auto and home-equity transactions, however, is the interest-only security. Interest-only structuring often is especially appropriate with payment-stable assets, such as autos, where the perceived risk of purchasing such a potentially volatile security is lower.

Interest-only securities can increase net proceeds to the issuer and can be created when the coupon rate on the receivables pool is high relative to the sum of the market-driven coupon on the securities, ongoing transaction expenses, and the amount of excess servicing required for credit enhancement. Of course, another way to increase net proceeds is to issue premium securities with high coupons. Premium securities can possess additional prepayment risk relative to par securities and may be less desirable to investors, which may cause the spread on those securities to widen. Instead, this cash flow can be allocated to an interest-only security. Although the spread to Treasuries on the interest-only security may be relatively wide, this spread only will apply to a very small security; conversely, a wider spread on the entire transaction would apply to a larger amount of cash flow, potentially creating a higher all-in financing cost.

Interest-only securities can be issued as strips (that may carry a high degree of the prepayment risk of the underlying collateral) or as planned-amortization-class (PAC) securities (that contain less prepayment risk). PAC securities generally are structured to pay according to a pre-specified schedule as long as underlying prepayments remain constant and within a pre-specified band.

In its PAC form, the interest-only security generally is sized such that, as long as prepayments remain below the upper level of the band, investors will not be exposed to yield reduction (interest is not paid on prepaid assets in the pool). Depending on the transaction's structure, investors, however, may have an upside if prepayments go below the lower band. The planned-amortization security is senior in prepayment priority to a companion security (which may be the residual interest in the pool and is backed, at least partially, by excess spread from the underlying assets). In general, the higher (lower) the upper band, the lower (higher) the proceeds, but the lower (higher) the yield and spread to comparable Treasuries. By establishing the upper band at a higher level, investors are protected against fast pool prepayments. As a general matter and depending on transaction specifics, as the lower band goes down, investors may require a higher yield. This is because their chance of "upside" from additional cash flow resulting from slow prepayments may be diminished.

EMBEDDED OPTIONS AND FLOATING-RATE MISMATCH

Underlying assets can be based on different indices than the securities that they support. Fixed-rate assets can back floating-rate securities (or visa versa). Adjustable-rate assets (assets that float according to an index, but may be limited by periodic or lifetime caps and floors, as well as teased initial rates) can back floating-rate securities (which, of course, may also be subject to specific caps and/or floors). Assets that float based on one index (for example, the prime rate) can back securities that float based on another (for example, LIBOR). Such structures often are created to address specific investor demands or allocate risk to particular parties. Several issues, however, must be considered when structuring such securities:

- Tax implications are important. Competent tax counsel should carefully examine the structure. Mismatches generally will work in debt-for-tax, REMIC, or FASIT structures.
- Credit enhancement considerations are paramount. If excess servicing is compromised due to market movements, less cash flow may be available to credit enhance the securities.
- The risk in such "mismatch" transactions often is largely allocated to the issuer's retained interest. The issuer should carefully analyze this risk.
- Options and/or swaps can be used to hedge or mitigate mismatch risk. The cash flow of these derivative instruments can be allocated to investors or, conversely, an issuer may wish to retain them "outside of the transaction" to manage its own risk.

Often, an "available-funds cap" is placed on the securities. In such a case, the rate paid to security holders never can exceed a certain rate, generally based on the rate that the underlying assets pay minus ongoing expenses and any "cushion" that may be required by credit enhancers. When an available-funds cap is used, the investor is generally short an interest-rate option(s). In certain markets, due to inefficiencies in pricing risk, the present value of the implied yield premium demanded by investors for this short position exceeds the price at which such an option can be purchased from a third party. In these scenarios an arbitrage opportunity exists, and options can be purchased and imbedded in the security, a process that raises several structuring challenges.

Embedding options and swaps not only raises tax and other legal issues (for example, ERISA considerations or SEC registration requirements), but also potentially introduces prepayment and credit risk. For example, it may be difficult to structure such instruments to amortize with the notional value of a pool, which itself is subject to prepayment risk.[8] Also, the holder of such instruments is exposed to the credit risk of the counterparty (and the counterparty may need to publicly disclose information that it does not wish to disclose). Furthermore, should payments be required by the holder (for example, in a swap contract), the availability of such cash flows and their effect on the payments due security holders should be analyzed.

Public versus Private Execution

Securities can be issued in the public or private markets. Public securities are registered pursuant to The Securities Act of 1933 (the "Act"). Privately placed asset-backed transactions generally are issued in transactions exempt from the Act.[9] Within the private placement market, three general types of transactions exist: (1) transactions pursuant to Rule 144A, which may enjoy more liquidity than traditional privately placed securities; (2) traditional private placements; and (3) confidential private placements, which usually involve confidentiality agreements executed with potential investors and other parties.

In general, issuers consider the following issues when deciding the market in which to issue:

- Public securities are often more liquid and generally trade at lower yields. This is especially true of larger transactions, higher rated securities, and assets that are well understood by the market.
- Public securities may include greater up-front expenses, such as Securities and Exchange Commission fees (currently $\frac{1}{29}$ of 1% of the principal balance of the offering) and financial printing (this is really an optional expense; some public issuers are now photocopying prospectuses).[10]
- Public securities historically have been more prone to unsolicited credit ratings.
- For non-generic transactions, the private market can sometimes offer the most efficient execution because of the ability of investors to have greater involvement in documentation and transaction structuring and the lack of liquidity advantage such transactions may otherwise have in the public markets.

---

[8] If it is not possible to make the notional value of the option amortize with the pool's actual performance, the option's notional amortization schedule can be set as a zero-prepayment schedule (which may be costly) or at a very slow prepayment schedule (which introduces risk to investors to the extent that the pool actually pays at a rate slower than that used in projecting the schedule).

[9] Transactions issued by "exempt issuers" (for example, a bank) generally are not exempt from the Act in the asset-backed markets. This is because the trust, not the issuer, is considered the registrant of the securities for Act purposes. Note, however, that credit enhancement, such as a surety bond or option contract, is considered a security. If such enhancement is from a non-exempt issuer, it may be subjected to registration requirements.

[10] Many people are under the impression that a public transaction is more difficult to document than a private placement (thereby running up more legal time). This is arguable and may not even be the case at all. The documentation requirements for most asset-backed transactions are pretty much the same whether the securities are offered on a public or private basis, and generally consist of a set of principal contracts to establish the asset pool, issue the securities, and provide for servicing, as well as an offering document.

- Private transactions can be executed confidentially. Typically, offering documents contain information relating to a company's underwriting guidelines or other statistics (for example, customer concentrations in trade receivables financings), that an issuer may not want to put in the public domain.
- Private transactions can be more easily amended or restructured subsequent to issuance.
- Private transactions often subject the issuer to risks of delayed closing due to investor negotiations. Sometimes (but, of course, not generally) private transactions subject the issuer to the risk of re-negotiated pricing or structuring between the dates of pricing and closing.

In late 1992, the Securities and Exchange Commission made the public offering of asset-backed securities considerably easier when it broadly allowed for asset-backed shelf registration statements. The rules permitting asset-backed shelf registrations have generally mitigated "SEC review risk" (i.e., the risk that the SEC will fully review a potential public offering, thus potentially subjecting the issuer to delay). Another result of the asset-backed shelf rules has been the establishment of underwriter shelves, also called "rent-a-shelves." In a "rent-a-shelf" transaction, the originating seller/servicer sells its assets to the entity that has previously established an asset-backed shelf (often an affiliate of the underwriter). The "rent-a-shelf" concept allows an infrequent issuer that would like to do a public offering that cannot itself justify the time and expense necessary to establish a shelf registration statement to access efficiently the public markets. In addition, shelves reduce cost by eliminating the requirement of delivering red herrings and creating de novo documentation for subsequent offerings. They further potentially familiarize potential investors with upcoming offerings; they help investors to be knowledgeable about the issuer's shelf in general.

Tax Efficiency

The major tax law consideration in structuring pools is often to avoid creating an entity for federal income tax purposes that is treated like a corporation. The technical term for such an entity is an "association taxable as a corporation." A corporation in the United States (other than a closely held "S corporation") is taxable as a legal entity separate from its owners. This can be distinguished from, for example, a partnership, in which the income is attributable to the partners and not to the entity that is the partnership.

REMIC legislation allows a corporate type of entity — not necessarily a corporation but an entity for corporate law purposes, such as a corporation, a partnership, or a trust — to elect to be treated as a REMIC for federal income tax purposes. Most REMICs are trusts. However, if one had a particular result in mind and created a mortgage-backed security issuer as a corporation in form and had that corporation elect to be treated as a REMIC (or a FASIT, should the pending legislation be adopted), the REMIC election would supersede the general rule that a corporation's income is subject to a corporate tax.

A REMIC is not an entity. Instead, it is a tax election that an entity may make. Although it is perhaps not so confusing to see this with REMICs, the confusion becomes much greater when other types of federal tax law constructs, for example, partnerships, are considered. A partnership is both a federal income tax law status as well as a corporate entity concept. For example, a partnership for state partnership law purposes could elect to be treated as a REMIC for tax purposes; further, a trust for state corporate purposes may elect to be treated as a partnership for tax purposes.

On May 9, 1996, the IRS issued proposed regulations that simplify the process for determining if an entity will be treated as a corporation or a partnership for tax purposes. Under the proposed regulations, certain types of state law and foreign entities will be treated as per se corporations. All other entities can elect to be treated as either partnerships or as corporations with the additional provision that entities that do not make an election will "default" into partnership status. A trust created as a securitization vehicle would therefore default to partnership status if the IRS were to determine that it did not qualify as a trust for tax purposes.

These proposed "check-the-box" regulations will apply for periods beginning after the date the regulations are issued in final form. IRS officials have stated that they expect to issue final regulations by the end of this year. The current "four factor test" for classifying entities will continue to apply until the proposed regulations become final. The proposed regulations state, however, that the IRS will not challenge the characterization of existing entities for periods which the current rules apply if the entity had a reasonable basis for its claimed classification.

The four factor test refers to the requirement under current IRS regulations that to be regarded as a partnership an entity must lack at least two of four characteristics not common to both corporations and partnerships. These characteristics are continuity of life, centralization of management, limited liability, and free transferability of interests. After the "check-the-box" regulations become final, trusts drafted to have a partnership fallback will not have to meet the four factor test requirements. Further, existing entities will then be able to drop partnership fallback provisions and still claim partnership status if their characterization as a trust is successfully challenged by the IRS.

The rules regarding publicly traded partnerships, however, have not been changed. Partnerships treated as publicly traded partnerships are taxed as corporations. Therefore, to avoid taxation as a corporation, an effective partnership fallback will continue to require provisions restricting the total number of holders of equity or deemed equity interests in order to avoid publicly traded partnership status upon a recharacterization of the trust.

As a general matter, when legislators created technical rules relating to whether or not a particular entity is treated as an "association taxable as a corporation" for federal income tax purposes, it appeared that they were attempting to prohibit multiple classes of ownership interests in one of these entities. As a general rule, the tax laws pretty much allow for only one class of equity interest to be issued in any of these entities. A REMIC, for example, is required to issue one and only one class of equity interests in itself, which is called the residual interest. A grantor trust, which is a tax election frequently used for asset-backed transactions involving types of non-revolving assets other than mortgages (such as auto loans), permits multiple classes of ownership but does not permit for the shifting of certain risks among the various classes of ownership. For example, one cannot as a general rule create a "sequential-pay" structure in a grantor trust, although through some rather intricate drafting one can come pretty close, but probably will not match the flexibility that can be achieved for mortgage securitizations that use a REMIC election. So as one moves away from mortgage loans as an asset class and into other types of assets (and does not use an efficient debt-for-tax structure), there may be many more restrictions that may effectively prohibit the dicing and slicing of the asset pool into the types of securities that one would ideally like to offer to feed particular investor appetites.

Almost all of these federal income tax restrictions that apply to asset pools other than mortgages are rules against multiple classes of ownership interests in the asset pool, or rules that narrowly prescribe the type of ownership interests that can be issued. In other words, the restrictions are restrictions on multiple classes of equity, as opposed to restrictions on multiple classes of debt. Therefore, many multi-class, non-mortgage transactions have been structured as the issuance of debt rather than the issuance of ownership interests in the form of certificates.

As discussed above, debt treatment is often difficult to achieve. This is the case even when the transaction is structured to be debt in form. One of the principal difficulties in structuring debt, of course, is the necessity of having a class of equity from which we can distinguish the debt. Using equity to distinguish debt often is used in what is commonly called an "owner trust." An owner trust basically works as follows: a trust is created and capitalized with the receivables pool. The trust then issues certificates of equity ownership in itself. The trust then also effectively enters into an indenture and issues debt. The debt of the trust typically is sold to third-party investors as rated, fixed-income securities. The equity ownership in the trust may be retained by the company, or a portion may also be sold to investors. As long as such a transaction is structured to comply with SFAS 77, it may be accounted for as a GAAP sale.

There are few or no restrictions on the type of debt that an owner trust may issue. Therefore, the debt (if it is properly characterized as debt) may, for example, be structured as a "sequential pay" series of notes. One of the trade-offs that should be evaluated by an issuer of non-mortgage, non-revolving assets would then generally be the following: is it more advantageous to use an owner trust/debt structure that allows for the carving up of the asset pool into multiple classes of debt, thus allowing its investment bank to target specific investors with narrowly constructed securities, but suffer the downside that an economic equity interest must now be created and presumably held? Or, should it structure the transaction as the sale of pass-through equity interests in the issuing trust, recognizing that the types of securities that can be created may not be specifically targeted to individual investors due to the more restrictive provisions of federal income tax law relating to the creation of multiple classes of ownership?

Deal Size

A larger transaction, other things being equal, provides scale economies and more structuring opportunities to allow for the targeting of specific investors and enhanced liquidity. Transaction sizes can be increased through two distinct avenues: pre-funding accounts and the issuance of joint securities through securitization conduits.

Pre-Funding Accounts

A pre-funded transaction generally allows the issuer to close the securitization when only part of the collateral can be delivered to the trustee. The trustee then holds some of the cash proceeds in an account (the pre-funding account) and releases that cash to the issuer when and if subsequent collateral is delivered within a specified time period. Although the issuer is not contractually obligated to deliver the pre-funding collateral, issuers generally feel not only a moral obligation to do so, but also understand the importance of doing so if they wish to issue subsequent pre-funded transactions and have them accepted by the market.

Subsequent deliveries must materially conform to a pool description that is disclosed to investors in the offering document. If this collateral is not delivered to the trustee by the issuer, the cash in the pre-funding account is paid to investors. The transaction's operative documents will specify how this cash would be allocated among investor classes. For an established issuer that can be expected to materially fill the pre-funding account, a pre-funded deal (with a reasonably sized pre-funding account) should trade (and generally does) comparably to a transaction that has all of the collateral on the closing date.

Other considerations of pre-funded transactions are as follows:

- The issuer and its banker should carefully consider how the final pool will be parametized. Defining the pool too narrowly inhibits flexibility; yet, defining it too broadly deteriorates marketability.
- The pre-funding account effectively allows an issuer to hedge its production because the funding cost of the subsequent deliveries has been set at the time of pricing.
- The pre-funding period must be carefully tailored. If it is too short, it may make it difficult for the issuer to deliver the additional collateral. If it is too long, it may increase cost, and supplemental interest would have to be funded into a capitalized interest account to cover potential shortfalls between the yield on the cash investments in the pre-funding account and the bond coupon. Maximum terms also are effectively set by the REMIC rules for mortgage collateral. A subtle point is that, as the allowable pre-funding period increases, investors may make longer average-life assumptions, as newly originated collateral could be delivered at a later date.

- The pre-funding account gives the originator more flexibility in timing the market, as securities can be sold prior to the full formation of a pool.
- The pre-funding account gives the originator enhanced flexibility for determining how much collateral to sell in a given period. Subsequent deliveries can take place within the same accounting period as the initial sale, thereby allowing GAAP sales treatment for a greater amount of collateral within a given period.
- Careful legal analysis should be conducted. For example, as of this writing, certain ERISA considerations apply to prefunded transactions.

Conduits

The word "conduit" has yet to develop any single meaning. Yet it generally refers to the idea that smaller originators who lack name recognition in the capital markets and scale economies may still access the securitization market by entering into conduit relationships with larger, more seasoned issuers. One distinguishing characteristic of conduit relationships is the extent to which a participant retains an ongoing interest in its loans. Some conduits buy whole loans, usually at a premium, such that they purchase the receivables pool entirely from the smaller originator. Other conduits purchase the receivables pool at its par and give the participant an ongoing interest in its loans over time, thus paying out the premium on an as-earned basis.[11] The latter conduit relationship is similar to the idea of a conduit participant issuing its own asset-backed securities by "piggy backing" its asset pool onto the asset pool of a larger originator. These structures are in fact referred to as "piggy-back securitizations." A second distinguishing characteristic of conduit relationships is whether or not they allow for the retention of servicing by the originator, to the extent that the originator or an affiliate thereof is itself a servicer.

STRUCTURING DEALS — A GENERAL APPROACH

The investment banker must understand both issuer objectives and current investor preferences. To structure an efficient transaction, he must optimize the trade-offs between both and be knowledgeable about the constantly evolving intricate rules briefly highlighted herein.

Not every problem ultimately will be solvable. Yet, most structuring problems can be overcome or at least alternatives can be proposed. Then the issuer can decide whether or not to pursue one strategy over the other.

Creativity is critical, and structuring asset-backed securities offers a myriad of opportunities to be creative. But before a banker or lawyer can suggest creative options, they first must master the technical details, which requires years of

---

[11] Combinations of these methods can be used. For example, a modest premium could be paid at closing and a reduced amount of ongoing cash flow could be passed through during the time that the securitization is outstanding.

specialization and seasoning. A less desirable approach is to study one, two, or at most a small number of prior transactions to use as a model for the transaction that they have been asked to structure. This generally produces inefficiencies; if you study only several models you tend to think of those models as embodying rules rather than as being examples of what can be accomplished given a particular set of evolving constraints and opportunities.

Chapter 3

Non-Traditional Asset Securitization for European Markets

Joseph D. Smallman
Managing Director
London Branch
Vining-Sparks IBG

Michael J. P. Selby, Ph.D.
Centre for Quantitative Finance
Imperial College of Science, Technology and Medicine, London, U.K.
and
The Financial Options Research Centre
The University of Warwick, Coventry, U.K.

INTRODUCTION

Twenty-five years ago the markets for Eurodollar and securitized instruments were in their infancy. Both of these markets have shown phenomenal growth through financial innovation. A key element contributing to the growth of the securitization market has been the demand by investors, especially European ones, for floating-rate instruments. As these products evolved, their spreads have tightened, thus creating an opportunity for "non-traditional" securitized instruments.

Traditionally, mortgages, credit card receivables, and automobile loans, for example, are securitized in the United States for global distribution. These securities are issued in both fixed and floating-rate form. When originally issued, the spread for both mortgage-backed and asset-backed securities was relatively large. The pricing was a reflection of the innovative nature of the products. Today, these are seasoned products in a well-developed liquid market, trading at tight spreads.

To satisfy the demand for wider spreads, "non-traditional" asset classes are making their way to the market. In 1996 Standard & Poor's published a review and discussed the new criteria used for rating several of these "non-traditional" assets, such as tax liens, non-performing consumer loans, 12-b(1) fees (a fee

45

some mutual funds receive), franchise loans, rental car fleets, and small business loans.[1]

We shall address both dollar and non-dollar denominated securities, paying special attention to those based on U.S. dollar assets. Initially, some of the procedures described in this chapter, and used to securitize non-traditional U.S. assets for European markets, may seem strange. However, European financial institutions differ in a number of important ways from the rest of the world. Consequently, the structuring of securitized products must reflect the demands of European-based investors, which do not necessarily exist in other markets such as North America. The satisfaction of the desires, tastes, needs and preferences of the European financial market explains why non-standard approaches are being used to overcome international obstacles, especially those due to government and other regulation.

This chapter is organized as follows. Because of the importance of Eurodollar instruments, we describe first the relationship between the Eurodollar market and the United States domestic financial market. We then focus on "non-traditional" securitized instruments, paying particular attention to the needs of European investors. In order to demonstrate how innovative and diverse the securitization market has become, we describe three types of instruments in some detail — instruments based on U.S. small business loans, royalties and patent income, and export future-flows receivables.

THE EURODOLLAR MARKET VERSUS THE U.S. DOMESTIC MARKET

The European U.S. dollar market provides a unique opportunity for placing many "non-traditional" U.S. dollar assets via securitization. Before we describe some of the new types of instruments, which have been created to securitize these assets for European investors, it is important to compare and contrast the U.S. market with the European market.

The European U.S. dollar market, more commonly called the Eurodollar market, refers to all U.S. dollars invested outside the United States. The evolution of this market began during the Cold War between the Soviet Union and the United States. The Soviets feared that the U.S. authorities would freeze or hold the deposits that they had with the Federal Reserve Bank. To eliminate this problem, the Soviets lent these dollars to Commercial de l'Europe du Nord located in Paris and the Moscow Narodny Bank in London. This practice of moving U.S. dollars offshore away from U.S. domestic regulations, like Regulation Q which capped lending rates, was quickly adopted by other European merchant and U.S. banks. Thus the birth of the Eurodollar market.

---

[1] *Structured Finance Ratings Asset-Backed Securites Beyond the Traditional Asset Classes: New Assets '96* Standard & Poor's October 1996.

According to the International Securities Market Association (ISMA),[2] the dollar remains the largest denomination in the Euromarkets. In 1996 the market increased over the previous year's issues by over $100 billion to a total of $270 billion, with total market size being $1.457 trillion by the end of the year. Much of this growth came from the increased issuance of asset-backed securities, with more than $80 billion being issued in 1996.

One may very well ask why so many U.S. dollar assets are finding a home in Europe? The European financial market is made up of various countries with different currencies, languages, and cultures. The European Community is working on eliminating this first difference by introducing the euro, formerly called the European Currency Unit (ECU). This is not to be confused with the Eurodollar. The ECU is a basket currency. From January 1, 1999 one "ECU" will equal one euro. The euro will eventually replace all the European Community countries' currencies.[3]

The U.S. dollar remains the currency of choice for European banks. It is an easy currency to convert into a home currency and to be the base currency for a variety of structured products, which simplifies lending, swapping or hedging. If one looks to all of the various markets, the U.S. dollar based market is the most liquid.

Many sovereign states and corporate entities borrow from banks and issue debt in U.S. dollars; however most, if not all, consumer debt is in the home currency. Therefore, there does not exist a naturally matched asset base as there is in the United States (e.g. mortgages, credit cards, auto loans, etc.). In spite of this, the market for Eurodollars is both large and efficient, even though there does not exist a natural underlying base for U.S. dollar denominated assets.

European and U.S. banks also differ in the way in which they run their treasury operations. Most European banks match funds. That is to say, they fund their assets to match their liabilities. For example, if it is planned to lend a corporation $100 million, an adjustable-rate loan indexed to the 3-month London Interbank Offer Rate (LIBOR) will usually be issued. If the company requires a fixed-rate loan, then the bank will swap it into a floating-rate one. To fund the loan the bank will borrow at 3-month LIBOR. The spread between the funding cost and lending rate will be the profit. Banks are indifferent to changes in interest rates because their funding cost moves lock-step to their receivables. Just as they lend, so they invest.

The floating-rate note (FRN) market is very active in Europe and has shown remarkable growth, more than doubling in size in 1996, with new issuance exceeding $1.4 billion compared to only $600 million in 1995.[4] This explains why U.S. dollar asset-backed and mortgage-backed floating-rate securities are so actively traded in the Eurodollar market; they easily fit into a European bank's balance sheet. In contrast, most U.S. banks lend and invest at fixed rates.

---

[2] Clive Horwood, *Quarterly Comment*, Vol. 28, January 1997, p. 6.

[3] Graham Bishop, Jose Perez, and Sammy van Tuyll, *The User Guide to the Euro*, Federal Trust, 1996, pp. 29-31.

[4] *Bank for International Settlements – 67th Annual Report*, p. 129.

EUROPE GOING FORWARD

The traditional U.S. dollar assets that are traded in European markets are floating-rate instruments such as U.S. corporate bonds, asset-backed credit cards, floating-rate CMO tranches, and floating-rate U.S. agency paper. According to Moody's Investors Service, European asset-backed securities (ABS) issuance is expected to jump 25% in 1998 to the high $40 billion range (including private deals).[5] Furthermore, of all the international ABS deals done in 1997, 70% were in U.S. dollars. As the demand for ABS grows in Europe, it is natural for "non-traditional" U.S. dollar assets to find their way to the market. We have listed assets that have been placed recently in the European markets:

U.S. Small Business Administration loans	Project finance
Music royalties	Housing Association mortgages
Oil	Equipment leases
Ships	Service station receivables
Bond backed	Nursing homes receivables
Corporate loans	Steel receivables
Leases	Road tolls
Commercial mortgages	Copper exports receivables
Student loans	Gold exports receivables
Trade receivables	Insurance notes

To describe each of these assets individually is beyond the scope of this chapter. However, by describing securitized instruments based on U.S. SBA Guaranteed Loan Pools Certificates, royalties and patent income cash flows, and export receivables future-flow transactions, we believe that the reader will gain a good view of just how diverse this market is.

U.S. SBA GUARANTEED LOAN POOLS CERTIFICATES

One asset class European investors have found attractive is U.S. Small Business Administration Guaranteed Loan Pools Certificates (SBA GLPC).[6] To illustrate one way "non-traditional" U.S. dollar assets are placed in Europe, we are going to review how the SBA GLPC are being securitized for European clients.

Most ABS are overcollateralized. The special purpose vehicle (SPV) that holds the assets and issues the security normally has a face value smaller than the aggregate principal value of the collateral. The reason for this is that in most, if not all cases, the credit quality of the collateral is lower than the credit rating of the ABS. The overcollateralization serves to absorb any delays and defaults. In contrast, when securitizing premium SBA GLPC the structures are under collateralized! Since the U.S. government guarantees the SBA GLPC and issues the currency, there is no higher level of credit. If the U.S. government fails, so does the

---

[5] *Asset Sales Report International*, Vol. 1, Issue 2, March 9, 1998 p. 13.
[6] When we refer to "pools" we are referring to the SBA GLPC.

currency. The extremely high credit rating of the U.S. government, combined with the fact that most SBA GLPC have high coupons, enables the instruments to usually trade at a premium to their face value. As a result, the securitized instrument is issued at par, with the underlying collateral priced at a premium. This creates an undercollateralized instrument. By securitizing a large portfolio of premium priced pools via an offshore grantor trust, the originators transform SBA GLPC into an investment suitable for European investors. This product is one of the first securitizations that we are aware of that is undercollateralized.

ROYALTIES AND PATENT INCOME

The increasing transparency in the foreign exchange markets due to the creation of the euro is expected to lead to a general increase in the issuance of securitized instruments by European and other issuers. This should prove particularly attractive to multinational firms such as those in the entertainment, pharmaceutical, and biotechnology industries, which will have the opportunity to securitize their royalties and patent income streams.

The entertainment industry is already proving to be a fruitful non-traditional source for securitization instruments. What do David Bowie (David Robert Jones) and Rod Stewart have in common? If you said that they are both English singers and song writers, born in the 1940s, you would be correct. This, however, is not the only thing which they have in common. Both have securitized their royalties income. In 1997 the securitization of Bowie's future-cash flows netted him $55 million. Further, as recently as the spring of 1998, Nomura Capital issued a $15 million securitized loan backed by income from Rod Stewart's music publishing catalogue. Similarly, it is also anticipated that film studios, for example, will soon securitize their royalties and other income based on blockbuster films, such as Titanic.

EXPORT RECEIVABLES FUTURE-FLOW TRANSACTIONS[7]

Since the latter half of 1997 investors have become increasingly nervous in regard to both Asian and emerging markets. A common characteristic of these markets is that they usually relate to economies with a very strong export sector. A large number of the economies are rich in natural resources and other commodities such as oil, gas, copper, textiles, etc. They also have in common that their sovereign risk will usually dominate their industrial and corporate risk, which then creates a ceiling in regard to the amount and type of debt any one country or producer is able to issue. Furthermore, there are frequently laws relating to export quotas and mandatory currency conversions. This is particularly true for the former eastern bloc countries such as those of the Commonwealth of Independent States (CIS).

---

[7] This section is substantially based on an article in *International Securitisation Report* No. 29, May, 1998, by Brian Noer. We thank Brian Noer for his advice and assistance in the production of this section.

As a means of overcoming these obstacles, proposals for the securitization of export receivables are reaching an advanced state of preparedness. Future-flow export receivables securitizations are essentially about keeping cash flows offshore before the debt is serviced. This is motivated by the fact that usually the exporter has a higher credit quality than that of the home sovereign state. If it is possible to uncouple the link between the producer and its sovereign state, then financial securities issued, and collateralized by export receivables transactions, will be rated independently of the home country.[8] Any reduction in control over export receivables is potentially beneficial, as a producer in a country with a volatile country rating, will be likely to have an otherwise excessive funding cost.

The obtaining of the desired reduction in governmental control is by no means trivial. In the case of Russia, for example, 50% of hard currency proceeds must be converted to roubles, and 100% of export proceeds must be remitted back to Russia within 30 days. The first regulation is a presidential decree, while the second is the result of national legislation. Similar laws exist in other countries. For example, in Turkey the remittance amount is 70% and the time period is 90 days.

These regulatory conditions are not insurmountable, providing that there are no fears concerning the possibility of subsequent government intervention, once a securitization has been put in place. Unfortunately, such fears do exist, and are likely to exist for the foreseeable future, given the 1980s third world debt crises experience. However, efforts are being made to obtain the necessary waivers and guarantees which need to be put in place, in order to create the appropriate SPVs.

It is generally considered to be only a matter of time before we see the first securitization based on export receivables future-flow transactions. The likelihood of a downturn in the world economy will actually increase the desirability of these instruments. Any move towards a global recession will cause a decrease in the demand for natural resources and other commodities. Countries heavily dependent on exports and external finance will then find that securitization of their export receivables transactions, and the associated regulatory adjustments, are the only way forward.

It is also worth noting that what is being proposed is not really new. One is essentially talking about commodity-backed bonds. These bonds were used extensively in North America in the 1860s. The Confederate States of America issued cotton-backed bonds during the War Between the States. Just as they were then, they are being used now to pierce a country's rating ceiling.

SUMMARY

In this chapter we have described how "non-traditional" asset classes are entering the Eurodollar market via securitization. We have shown that non-traditional

---

[8] In practice, even the most developed countries, such as the United Kingdom and the United States, usually have some influence over the activities of companies and other organizations incorporated under their jurisdiction.

methods may be required when dealing with "non-traditional" asset classes. In the case of the SBA GLPC it was necessary to use a combination of undercollateralization within a grantor trust structure to create a synthetic Eurodollar FRN. In contrast, royalties and patent income structures are relatively straightforward to create. However, export receivables future-flow transactions raise important legal and political issues and are likely to require special structuring.

It now seems clear that the role of securitization has not only moved on significantly from that of the mid 1980s, but it is almost certainly going to become, in our view, the principal conduit for most debt financing in the future, as the demand for ever greater liquidity increases.

Chapter 4

Finance Company Transactional Due Diligence

Len Blum
Managing Director
Asset-Backed Finance
Prudential Securities Inc.

Michael A. Mattera
Associate
Investment Banking
Prudential Securities Inc.

INTRODUCTION

Due diligence is the process of discovering and analyzing risks, as well as ascertaining that disclosure is adequate. Numerous parties are involved; their respective goals and concerns often are unique. Such parties include investment bankers, lawyers, credit enhancers, investors, rating agencies, accountants, and others. This chapter provides a brief overview of the process. It is not complete or a checklist; it is an overview. Furthermore, issues will vary based on the originator, the servicer, the asset type, the transaction, the parties involved, and the perceived potential risks.

DESCRIPTIVE AND NORMATIVE DUE DILIGENCE

There are two types of due diligence: descriptive and normative. *Descriptive* due diligence is the process through which transaction parties ascertain that disclosure is accurate and complete. *Normative* due diligence focuses on ascertaining that risks are understood and potentially quantified.

Descriptive Due Diligence

The securities laws address descriptive due diligence in Section 17 (a) of the Securities Act of 1933, as amended (the "33 Act"), which states that "it shall be

The authors would like to thank Norman Chaleff of Prudential Securities and Rick Fried of Stroock & Stroock & Lavan for their input and guidance.

unlawful for any person in the offer or sale of any securities...to obtain money or property by means of any untrue statement of a material fact or any omission to state a material fact necessary in order to make the statements made, in the light of the circumstances under which they were made, not misleading."[1] Note that the Securities Act addresses disclosure only, not investment merit. Simply stated, for purposes of the 33 Act, material risk can exist if it is disclosed.

If a security is sold with an untrue statement or an omission of a material fact in its disclosure documentation, "any person acquiring a security registered under the Registration Statement may, pursuant to Section 11 (a) of the 33 Act, sue the issuer, its directors, its principal executive and financial officers, certain experts who participate in preparation of the Registration Statement, and each underwriter."[2] Moreover, liability is absolute: "In connection with a Section 11 cause of action, it is not necessary to prove 'intention' or 'knowledge' with respect to the misstatement or omission..."[3] This means that, for an officer or director of the registrant, even if the statements were made in good faith, if they are untrue, those parties still will be liable.[4]

Non-issuer parties also should ascertain that disclosure is adequate. First, this is good business practice. Second, due diligence may provide a defense against disclosure liability for defendants other than the issuer. For example, an underwriter may avoid disclosure liability if "... a reasonable investigation is conducted, resulting in reasonable grounds to believe, and actual belief by the underwriter, that the registration statement is accurate and valid."[5] "In determining... what constitutes reasonable investigation and reasonable grounds for belief, the standard of reasonableness shall be that required of a prudent man in the management of his own property."[6]

Normative Due Diligence

Normative diligence addresses three issues: risk dynamics, investment appropriateness, and return adequacy. Descriptive diligence is a task for issuers, lawyers, "experts," and underwriters; normative diligence involves additional parties:

- Rating agencies ascertain that ratings adequately describe risk.
- Bankers and investors[7] verify that risks are understood, fairly priced, and appropriate.

---

[1] *SEC Handbook, Volume 1: Securities Act of 1933*, Section 17(a), RR Donnelley Financial International Printing Services, 1996.

[2] *Outline of Due Diligence Investigation Procedures.* Segment of section 11(a) of the Securities Act of 1933.

[3] "Due Diligence: Some Basic Considerations," Stroock & Stroock & Lavan, October 1996.

[4] For purposes of the 33 Act liability, the sponsor of the trust has absolute liability, even though a trust (or other issuance vehicle) may be the literal issuer.

[5] *SEC Handbook, Volume 1: Securities Act of 1933*, Section 11(c).

[6] Ibid.

[7] As used hereinafter, the term "investors" applies to both purchasers of securities and credit enhancers.

Normative diligence fundamentally means constructing the logic chain that leads to the conclusion that, based on facts known at the offering, the investment should perform appropriately to its risk-adjusted pricing, and verifying appropriate chain links. Descriptive diligence is affected by normative diligence; the construction of the chain clarifies what issues should be covered by disclosure. The standard of descriptive due diligence is whether the information would materially affect an investor's decision to participate.

ARCHITECTURE AND DUE DILIGENCE

The transaction's architects must understand the potential risks involved. Structuring is often the optimal response to a risk, especially when structure can mitigate risks to an investor without imposing burdensome costs to an issuer. In other words, structure sometimes can maximize aggregate (for all parties), risk-adjusted present value.

One example of a structural element that addresses specific risk is the "trigger" event. Triggers require that certain procedures occur if prespecified "events" happen. These events are early-warning signs that risk may be increasing. For example, servicing triggers often specify that if a significant deterioration in asset quality, servicing performance, or servicer financial strength occurs, the servicer may be replaced. The documents may further require the backup servicer to be ready to act quickly (a so-called "hot backup"). Accordingly, the hot backup may receive tape updates, and other procedures may occur. If participants believe that servicing risk is manageable, a "cold backup" could be used. A cold backup would take longer to act than a hot backup; therefore, this provision addresses a lower-risk situation.

Collateral triggers can be useful, especially when parties disagree about the risk of pool deterioration. Such triggers can require increased enhancement when it is most needed (for example, by increasing the then-current reserve requirements) or take the form of an early-amortization event.

Outside-event triggers can address specific risks. In a Prudential Securities airline-ticket securitization, for example, an early-amortization event addressed labor-stoppage risk. In the event of a strike, significant pool dilution could occur. Because the Railway Labor Act requires a cooling-off period before a labor stoppage, we addressed this risk by making the inception of a cooling-off period an early-amortization event. This provided a safety net to investors if and when the likelihood of a strike increased.

Concentration limits often are established during due diligence. For example, in a timeshare transaction, the risk of foreign obligors may be identified. Foreign obligors may be risky because of sovereign considerations; and because the receivables are denominated in United States dollars, currency fluctuations could result in increased foreclosure frequency. To address this risk, limits on the aggregate amount of foreign borrowers or borrowers from any one foreign country or specific countries may be used.

INVESTIGATIVE SCOPE

Prior to on-site diligence, gather and analyze general information, list potential risks, and construct a list of contact parties (based on the identified risks). As parties are interviewed and information is gathered, more questions are likely to arise, or new risks may surface. Due to these considerations (and because each transaction is unique), it is inadvisable to have an all inclusive "due diligence list". Instead, questions often arise due to prior inquiry. Careful, active listening skills, experience, and, most of all, common sense are the keys to successful diligence.

Any material risk should be identified and analyzed. This analysis occurs on numerous levels. For example, the selection of credit enhancers, servicers, trustees, and other parties affects the risk profile. The legal, regulatory, economic, and demographic environment also should be considered. The collateral pool also may possess unique risks; it should be stratified and analyzed. Furthermore, a variety of parties may conduct analysis. It is not unusual to rely on "experts." As discussed later in this chapter, accountants, lawyers, appraisers, contract underwriters, and other specialists often are utilized.

TRADE-OFFS: DILIGENCE VERSUS REPRESENTATIONS AND WARRANTIES

If a creditworthy party gives representations and warranties about specific aspects of a transaction, it alleviates concern about those issues. Representations and warranties also can accelerate and/or lower the cost of diligence. Note that issuers often give representations which they are not 100% sure are factual. Why would a party do this? Because representations shift liability; often the only remedy for a breached representation is the repurchase of the affected receivable. So, in planning due diligence, examine representations, warranties, and the sponsor's creditworthiness. Obviously, any risk factors not covered by a creditworthy entity should be diligenced more carefully.

Representations and warranties often are negotiated during structuring. Negotiations regarding specific representations (as well as, in more limited cases, certain affirmative and negative covenants) can occur for a variety of reasons. As discussed, creditworthy risk assumption can significantly accelerate diligence, reduce costs, and shift liability. To transact quickly, a sponsor may grant fairly comprehensive representations. On a more subtle level, the sponsor may grant specific representations (or potentially limited guarantees[8]) to lower cost. Because more risk is retained, less is assumed by investors. And pricing is affected by the risk/reward relationship.

---

[8] Guarantees often are limited to enhance bankruptcy remoteness.

OFFSET DYNAMICS

After an asset is sold in a securitization, events can occur that may reduce the amounts that can be collected. This situation can occur when an obligor has an offsetting claim against the creditor arising from returns, contractual provisions (such as prompt-pay discounts or price-protection agreements), defective merchandise, or other liabilities. Furthermore, risks of legislative and case-law change should be understood. Practical offset often relates to debtor satisfaction. Note that channel dynamics affect risk; for example, if auto loans are purchased from an inadequate dealer, offsets may be significant. Concentrations (both obligor and channel) also affect offset. For example, private-label credit cards with significant retailer concentration(s) have greater risk than bank cards.

THE FALLACY OF BANKRUPTCY REMOTENESS

In securitizations, the "issuer" is, in a sense, the single purpose entity that holds the asset pool. Asset-backed transactions are expected to be bankruptcy remote. Generally, counsel issues an opinion that, in the event of a bankruptcy of the sponsor, the assets neither would or should be considered part of the sponsor's estate, nor would or should the issuer be substantively consolidated with the sponsor. This opinion is not considered law (as in a judicial opinion). Rather, it is the opinion of presumably reputable counsel. It also shifts some liability to the writer of the opinion (or their insurer).

Bankruptcy opinions do not address business risk. They are legal in nature. In reality, risk can increase if the sponsor or servicer (or other important party) becomes bankrupt and/or its credit deteriorates, even if the structure is legally bankruptcy-remote. For example, there may not be a creditworthy party from which to pursue remedies if representations are breached. Servicing may deteriorate or be expected to deteriorate; yet the bankruptcy court may be unwilling to allow servicer replacement. And transferring servicing in such an event could cause pool performance to deteriorate.

A bankruptcy of the seller/servicer can affect practical and legal offset risk. For example, bankruptcy can increase merchandise returns dramatically. If the credit of a sponsor's manufacturing affiliate deteriorates, the value of the underlying collateral and the willingness of obligors to pay may suffer.

Some parties conduct due diligence almost as if the transaction was an issuance of secured debt, not a bankruptcy-remote securitization. While this view may, in many instances, be extreme, it is logical: do not rely blindly on a legal opinion; instead, consider practical consequences of credit deterioration, and construct diligence accordingly.

MARKET DYNAMICS

Consider the market in which the company operates; business practices vary in different competitive environments. For example, subprime lenders currently operate in a market where speed of execution, amount of credit extended, loan tenor, and price often drive high-volume origination. Increasing execution speed beyond capacity, setting credit lines beyond a debtor's means or that which the collateral justifies, or reducing risk-adjusted pricing can spell disaster.

Channel dynamics can impact competitive factors. Wholesale or indirect channels can introduce risk or reduce profitability; originators/sellers[9] "shop" more than consumers do. Such originators/sellers often have an incentive to get the highest possible advance and/or the lowest effective yield. When many competitive buyers for paper exist, price-adjusted risk can increase.

Evaluate the potential for increased competition, and analyze the company appropriately. Barriers to entry and their sustainability can indicate how difficult it is for competition to increase. Expected market size also is important; competition can increase as growth slows. The entrance of securitization into an industry can attract competition.

These questions address market conditions and competition:

- What are the target markets and typical borrower profile(s)?
- What are the issuer's relevant market shares? Are they stable, growing or declining?
- What trends could affect the market (for example, marketing approach, products or services, litigation, government regulations, consolidations)?
- What are the seasonality/cyclicality/periodicity considerations?
- Where are the company's main geographical markets? Does management plan to expand or contract geographically? Why? Is competition geographically fragmented?
- Who are the major competitors for each product line, service or geographic region? How does the company compare?
- What sustainable (and temporary) advantages does the company have and what advantages do its competitors enjoy (for example, costs (for example, scale economies), methods of marketing (for example, cross-selling), expertise/experience, services, quality, and speed)?
- Are competitors expanding? Are competitors having difficulties?
- Is the business obligated by, or does it hold, any non-competition agreements? Have any recently expired or will soon expire?

---

[9] Examples of originators/sellers are dealers (manufactured housing and auto), mortgage brokers (home equity), contractors (home improvement), and developers (timeshares).

MANAGEMENT

It is impossible to overstate the importance of strong management. Management should have direct and relevant experience, preferably with the specific asset type and credit-grade being originated. All key departments — origination, finance, marketing, and servicing — should have experience and depth. Consider performing background investigations on and/or checking references for key personnel. Obtain organizational charts.

Strong incentives — tied to appropriate goals — are important. Inside ownership can provide an economic incentive and decrease the probability of management departures. Incentives should be tied to appropriate goals.

STRATEGY

Business strategy addresses the company's strengths, weaknesses, opportunities, and threats, as well as sources of sustainable competitive advantage (of both the company and its competitors). Business strategy must be understood to address cogently its implementation in functional areas (for example, marketing, underwriting, and servicing).

Channel and product diversification is an important part of strategy. But it can be a double-edged sword. Companies that "stick to their knitting" often are rewarded. Yet diversified originators sometimes enjoy more stable revenues and/ or possess enhanced ability to change. Geographic diversification can reduce risk by limiting exposure to regional trends.

FINANCIAL ANALYSIS

Much has been written about financial statement analysis; we will not belabor the point here. However, it is important to note that it is dangerous to apply standard formulas. For example, if the subject has lower capital ratios than the industry average, it does not mean that the company is undercapitalized. Such an analysis must consider the potential risks that the company faces, its potential growth, and its access to funds. Capital is a cushion for mistakes and risk. Therefore, riskier companies (or those with liberal accounting practices) need more capital. Capital also is a base for growth, and should be analyzed in light of the company's plans and opportunities. Ready access to capital and diversification of financing sources mitigates the effects of capital needs, as do other factors. Pay close attention to liquidity; liquidity crises are the single largest cause of finance company failures. Also examine asset and earnings quality (including assumptions used in capitalizing excess servicing and reserve adequacy).

Consider structural subordination. If separate corporate affiliates have varying access to capital, pay careful attention to each entity's responsibilities, including provisions of guarantees, representations, warranties, and indemnifications.

ORIGINATION

Origination areas include marketing, underwriting, collateral valuation (where applicable), and quality control. Determine whether marketing is effective, underwriting is logical and appropriately consistent, appraisals are reasonable, and quality is monitored. Loan quality cannot be analyzed in a vacuum. Risky loans are not bad, per se, if risks are understood, controllable, priced accordingly, and the originator can bear or lay off the risk.

Marketing

The following attributes are positive:

- Marketing procedures are consistent with the company's strategy.
- The company understands its borrowers; its marketing is targeted.
- The company maintains logical, current pricing guidelines.
- Borrower screening is efficient and thorough.
- Marketing is efficient and can adapt to change.

Focused marketing results from cogent strategy. The type of loan and borrower that the company's internal policies, processes, and systems accommodate also should be compatible with strategy.

Determine the current marketing activities and analyze changes. For example, if a company changes focus to lower-credit borrowers or reduces price, focus on the need for increased servicing efforts and effects on profitability.

Marketing should be flexible. Companies alter strategies, create new products, and attempt to meet changing customer needs. If the industry is changing and the company is not, asset quality and/or effective portfolio yield could be impacted.

The following questions assess marketing strategy:

- Who are the company's customers?
- What are their needs?
- How is each product sold and/or distributed (i.e., direct sales, third parties, direct mail, telemarketing)?
- How has this changed over time?
- Why do customers borrow from the company?

Other key aspects of market-strategy assessment include:

- Price/rebates/incentives.
- User-friendliness.
- Post-purchase service.
- Product offering.
- Advertising/effect of sales effort/market presence.
- Existing relationships/cross-selling.

UNDERWRITING

Understand the company's underwriting philosophy. What factors does it consider important? Does it use credit scoring, objective criteria and/or subjective criteria? It can be helpful to ask an underwriter to explain the analysis for a given group of loans.

Personnel and departmental organization are important. Analyze the background and experience of underwriters. In growing markets, experienced personnel are scarce, and experienced underwriters (and servicers) can be critical to quality. Effective approval authority should exist, and training should be adequate. If guideline exceptions are made, the process (including approval authority) should be reviewed.

Approval analysis should be crisp. Processing that is too rapid can cause portfolio deterioration. Conversely, if the issuer is slow or disorganized, frustrated, qualified borrowers may shop elsewhere, which may leave the issuer with customers that cannot otherwise borrow. Speed should be consistent with industry standards in light of the originator's efficiency.

Many companies purchase loans from other originators on bulk, minibulk or flow bases. Loans can be closed in the name of the originator or a third party. Each procedure creates its own particular risks.

Examine purchase procedures. Some originators re-underwrite all loans, while others use statistical samples. Both procedures can be appropriate. Also evaluate the procedures used to re-underwrite.

Compare purchase standards with retail criteria. If standards vary significantly, the company may be buying loans that it does not understand or cannot service appropriately.

Understand third-party procedures and standards for approving correspondents. A third party's experience, reputation, and financial viability can be reliable indicators of loan quality. Third-party actions also can affect performance. For example, home-improvement loans originated through contractors that stand behind their high-quality work perform. If quality is shoddy, borrowers may become frustrated and refuse to pay. Examine the following:

• Underwriting guidelines (which usually are published).
• Internal approval procedures.
• Consistency of underwriting standards.
• Procedures for overriding guidelines.
• Procedures for reviewing the appropriateness of underwriting criteria
• Process for valuing underlying collateral (if applicable).
• Internal quality control mechanisms in place (such as loan reunderwriting and verification of borrower information).

Approval rates address the conservatism of the underwriting process (as well as marketing focus). A relatively high approval rate may signal that a company has reduced underwriting standards to originate more loans.

The following questions address underwriting:

- Does the company underwrite subjectively or strictly to specified criteria? Is credit scoring used?
- What is the general philosophy and approach to pricing? What is documented? Does price compensate for risk?
- What are the normal terms given on loans? Are amortization periods, advance rates and documentation criteria rigid or only a starting point?
- Who is ultimately responsible for decisions?
- What is the background of a typical underwriter?
- Is there a training program?

COLLATERAL VALUATION

For certain products, particularly those enjoying liens on real properties, appraisal quality can be critical. Generally, the more the lender's underwriting policies rely on collateral, the more important it is to value that collateral correctly. Collateral reliance often increases (decreases) as borrower creditworthiness decreases (increases).

In home-equity lending, lenders generally use independent appraisers. This is appropriate. Regional expertise is required, and high loan volume is necessary to justify staff appraisers in many locations.

A formal process should exist to review each appraisers' experience, credentials, and reputation. All appraisers should be properly licensed and monitored. Appraisers should have knowledge of the property types with which and the areas in which they are working.

The company should maintain an "approved" appraiser list with requirements for remaining on that list. It should be clear what type of appraisal errors or other issues cause removal from the list.

Understand how appraisers are selected for particular loans. The individual or broker originating the loan should not exert control. During the quality control process, a random sampling of properties should be reappraised. Reappraisals should occur regularly, be analyzed by appraiser, and affect eligibility for the approved appraiser list.

QUALITY CONTROL

The quality control department is important; it monitors underwriting and appraisal quality. Additionally, the quality control department establishes policies for reviewing the conformity of new employees and third-party originators and monitors with industry standards and company guidelines. The quality control department should be staffed by experienced personnel and have a separate reporting function to avoid conflicts of interest. Internal quality control reports should be generated on a monthly basis, at minimum, and reviewed by senior management.

INTERNAL SYSTEMS

Systems diligence focuses on the accuracy, integration, and effectiveness of the system. A quality data processing system has the following attributes:

- Utilizes current technology.
- Is expandable to accommodate higher loan volume.
- Has adaptability.
- Meets servicing needs of the specific collateral.
- Is compatible with the origination arm and the servicing arm.
- Has appropriate backup and disaster recovery procedures.

An issuer with old technology is not necessarily in trouble, but it could be delaying purchases. Future changes could create a servicing interruption, which may negatively impact delinquencies.

SERVICING AND COLLECTIONS

Good servicers are oriented to their borrower types. In sub-prime lending, servicing is often the most crucial aspect of collateral performance. Sub-prime borrowers need proactive servicing, including frequent customer calls, follow-up, late notices and notification of intent to foreclose. A prime servicer may have difficulty adjusting to the focused approach required for sub-prime borrowers.

Servicers often are tested by the performance and loss mitigation of their serviced portfolio. The servicer should have experience servicing each particular type of product. A servicer incorporating a new product into its portfolio should be scrutinized closely due to lack of experience and potential systems shortfalls. A servicer proficient in one product type may not have immediate proficiency with another.

Increased sub-prime volume has created the need for large servicing platforms and increased staffing. Determine if the ratio of servicers and collectors to borrowers is within industry standards; however, note that a servicer can operate competently at a lower ratio if it is efficient.

Generally, tools and procedures that organize servicing and/or enhance information flow increase efficiency dramatically. One example is the automated, predictive dialing system. Another example is the tracking of borrower calls and servicing effectiveness.

Pay attention to the workout and collection effort. This group determines if borrowers are suitable for payment restructurings, or if foreclosures will maximize recovery. For example, with mortgage loans, payment restructurings may make more sense for loans with high loan-to-value ratios. Assistance should be provided to borrowers that are experiencing financial distress but are expected to ultimately recover. For example, in a small business loan the borrower may have suffered from an illness but the underlying business remains strong. Borrowers that seem unlikely to cure should be encouraged to sell the properties prior to foreclosure. Review statistics on the number of borrowers that adhere to restructurings.

Foreclosure and bankruptcy units should be experienced and have access to attorney networks. Examine the duration of the foreclosure process by state relative to industry standards. With mortgage loans, the effectiveness of the real estate owned group will affect loss severity. Properties should be sold in the shortest amount of time for the highest possible price. With auto loans, assess the disposition process. Time to sale and recovery rates should be reviewed and compared with industry standards.

The servicer may also have a responsibility in investor accounting and reporting. The servicer should understand the accounting group's responsibilities. If a master servicing arrangement exists, reporting must be crisp to allow the master servicer to review documents and remit appropriate funds to the trustee and, ultimately, the investor.

DATA ANALYSIS

Analyze the issuer/servicer's historical performance data, both on loan performance and prepayment levels. In particular, static pool analysis can offer tremendous insights. In such an analysis, specific loans, originated during a certain time period are isolated, and their performance is tracked. These pools isolate loan performance; growth and change in a dynamic pool can mask performance. For example, in a growing portfolio, if losses are lower early in a loan's life, losses will be understated.

Calculate expected loss and prepayment curves during static pool analysis. These can be used as vectors to estimate performance in stress scenarios.

Compare static pool data with industry standards. Also, understand a pool's behavior over time. For example, increased losses in certain months may be due to collateral deterioration. Decreased losses may be due to lower than expected loan-to-value ratios caused by collateral appreciation. Static pools from different time periods should be compared. If performance has changed from period to period, analyze the cause of the changes. It could be the result of changed underwriting guidelines, external factors, and/or servicing effects.

Understand definitions of delinquency and chargeoff. Not all companies apply the same definitions to these terms. Delinquencies can be on contractual or recency bases. Due dates relative to delinquency-measurement dates and definitions of delinquency tenor can affect performance data. Charge off policies (for example, a specified aging, foreclosure, or subjective judgment) can increase (decrease) delinquencies, thereby decreasing (increasing) periodic losses.

POOL ANALYSIS

Perform a data integrity check to ensure that loan-level information is accurate.[10] Pick a random sample of loan files and compare the data on the loan tape to the individual files. For certain assets or data fields, data will be tied to internal management reports (i.e., not the loan files). Check that these reports are credible. Consider verifying with borrowers that loans exist. For illustrative purposes, we have listed some of the data that should be checked in a typical home equity pool:

- Customer name.
- State in which the home collateral is located.
- Original loan amount.
- Interest rate (APR).
- Original number of payments.
- Amount of periodic payment.
- Original loan-to-value ratio.
- First payment date.

Aggregate values also are verified and comforted. The following is a general list of data in a home-equity transaction:

- The number and aggregate unpaid principal balance of loans in the pool.
- The number and aggregate unpaid principal balance of loans that were (a) originated by the issuer and (b) originated by third parties and purchased by the issuer.
- The number of states represented in the pool.
- The weighted-average term to scheduled maturity of the loans.
- The final scheduled payment date of the loan(s) with the latest maturity.
- The earliest and latest dates of origination.
- The lowest and highest term to scheduled maturity.
- The average outstanding principal balance.
- The weighted-average loan-to-value ratio at origination.
- The number of loans, the aggregate principal balance outstanding, and the percentage of the total pool by outstanding principal balance for each of the following tables:
  Geographical distribution of collateral.
  Years of origination.
  Distribution of original principal amount.
  Distribution of original loan-to-value ratios.
  Coupon rates.
  Remaining months to maturity.

---

[10] This can be done by a number of parties. If a surety is used, the bond insurer, as well as the accountants, will do the required verification. If a surety is not used, an outside accounting firm will perform the analysis alone.

- The greatest original loan amount and percentage it represents of the aggregate principal balance of the loans at origination.
- Comparison of the number of loans, dollar amounts, and percentages as listed under the following tables in the disclosure document to the corresponding information contained in or summarized from the general accounting records of the issuer:
  Loan origination.
  Loan servicing portfolio.
  Delinquency experience.
  Loan loss experience.

Accountants write "agreed-upon procedures" letters that compare the tape data with the information presented in the prospectus. Compare the transaction's statistics to previous pools originated by the issuer, the pools from which static performance curves were derived, and industry standards.

Lawyers are hired to give various opinions. To do this, lawyers conduct a legal review of official documents of the issuer such as the certificate of incorporation, by-laws, indentures, loan agreements, and other debt agreements. These agreements often contain negative covenants that can conflict with the securitization. In such event, appropriate consents or waivers may have to be obtained. In addition, legal counsel should examine thoroughly any past or pending litigation involving the issuing company. The importance of that litigation for disclosure should be decided by both counsel and the underwriter. All original-document information must agree with the information provided in the prospectus.

In addition, counsel should also opine that the proper corporate formalities have been addressed and that entering into the transaction does not conflict with any other agreement to which they are a party. The lawyers should also provide a 10b-5 opinion that the prospectus does not contain any untrue statement or an omission of a material fact.

Chapter 5

Rating Structured Securities

Andrew A. Silver, Ph.D.
Managing Director
Moody's Investors Service

INTRODUCTION

Credit ratings are becoming an increasingly important factor in structured finance markets around the world. As investors are faced with extremely complex securities from an ever-widening array of familiar and unfamiliar issuers in domestic and cross-border markets, they need a simple, unbiased, accurate, and globally consistent framework for analyzing credit risk. This chapter describes how the Moody's ratings process provides that framework to investors.

OVERVIEW

What is Structured Finance?

Structured finance is a term that evolved in the 1980s to refer to a wide variety of debt and related securities whose promise to repay investors is backed by (1) the value of some form of financial asset or (2) the credit support from a third party to the transaction.[1] Very often, both types of backing are used to achieve a desired credit rating.

Structured financings are offshoots of traditional secured debt instruments, whose credit standing is supported by a lien on specific assets, by a defeasance provision, or by other forms of enhancement. With conventional secured issues, however, it is generally the issuer's earning power that remains the primary source of repayment. With structured financings, by contrast, the burden of repayment on a specific security is shifted away from the issuer to a pool of assets or to a third party.

Securities supported wholly or mainly by pools of assets are generally referred to as either mortgage-backed securities (mortgages were the first types of assets to be widely securitized) or asset-backed securities, whose collateral backing may include virtually any other asset with a relatively predictable payment stream, ranging from credit card receivables or insurance policies to speculative-grade bonds or even stock. Outside the United States, both types of structured financing are often referred to simply as "asset-backed securities," which is the convention that we will employ here.

Cash Flow Structures — "Pass-Through" or "Pay-Through"

The support provided in structured financings can take on many forms. In transactions supported by assets, some or all of the cash flows from those assets can be dedicated to the payment of principal and interest. That type of transaction is known as a cash flow structure, which, in turn, may be structured in either of two ways: as a "pass-through" or as a "pay-through." (See Exhibit 1 for a schematic diagram outlining the major elements of a stylized cash flow transaction.)

Pass-through securities are equity instruments, in which the assets are typically sold to a trust. Investors buy shares of the trust and are entitled to interest at a specified pass-through rate of interest and to their share of principal payments.

Pay-throughs are debt obligations. The institution that wants to raise funds pledges or sells assets to a special-purpose, often bankruptcy-remote, "issuer," which issues notes or bonds.

In either type of cash flow structure, the cash flows to investors are secured primarily by the cash flows of the pledged assets. Issuers choose between the two types based on their accounting, tax, and regulatory needs.

Market Value Structures

In market value structures, the liquidation value of the assets is used to support the security. If investors are not paid by the issuer as promised, or if some other "trigger event" occurs (for example, if the market value of the collateral falls below a specified level), the collateral is sold in the secondary markets and investors receive repayment from the proceeds.

---

[1] In some countries, the term "securitization" is used synonymously with "structured finance."

Exhibit 1: Cash Flow Transaction
I. Loan Origination and Servicing

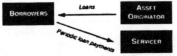

An *asset originator*, such as a bank, a savings bank, or a finance company, makes loans to *borrowers*. Borrowers repay the loans over time in periodic interest and principal payments. The repayments are typically administered by a *loan servicer*, which may be the same organization.

II. Adding the Transaction Structure

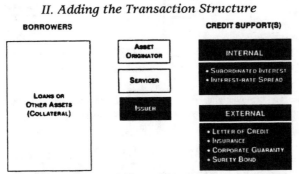

To sell/finance loans, the originator sets up a separate legal entity, the *issuer*. The issuer may be a special-purpose, bankruptcy-remote entity that issues debt, a trust that represents investors' interest in the assets, or another entity. The cash flow from the loans (i.e., the *collateral*) will be used to make interest and principal payments to investors. Credit enhancements may also be included to help reduce the risk of credit loss. These may be *internal*, provided by excess cash flow from the collateral, or *external*, such as a letter of credit from a bank or a financial guarantee from an insurance company.

III. The Securities Are Sold

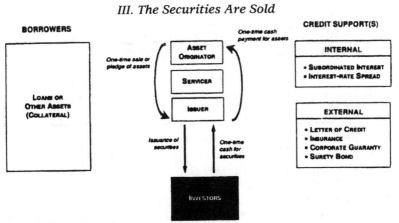

Investors purchase the securities by making a one-time payment to the issuer. The originator sells/pledges the assets to the issuer, who transfers the proceeds to the originator as a one-time payment for the assets.

Exhibit 1 (Continued)
IV. The Transaction's Cash Flows Over Time

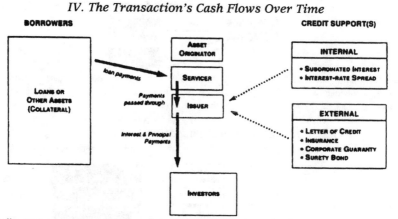

Generally, payments on the underlying collateral are the main source of cash to pay principal and interest. Borrowers continue to make periodic payments to the servicer and those payments are passed through to investors. If cash flow from the collateral is insufficient, then the credit supports may be drawn upon.

Exhibit 2: Market Value Transaction

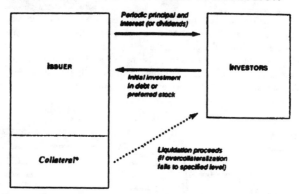

*Assets may be placed in a bankruptcy-remote, special-purpose corporation or held in trust accounts, or, in the case of a mutual fund, may be an unsegregated portion of the fund's assets.

There are three basic types of market value structures. In one structure, debt is backed by assets that are pledged to a trustee for the benefit of investors. In another structure, the assets are sold to a special-purpose, bankruptcy-remote issuer and then pledged as collateral for debt or preferred stock. In a third structure, debt or preferred stock is issued by an income (mutual) fund and the investors have a claim on all the assets of the fund. In the case of debt investors, that claim is senior to the (generally substantial) common equity interest in the fund, and in the case of preferred stock investors, the claim is senior to both the common equity and debt positions. (See Exhibit 2 for a schematic diagram outlining a stylized market value transaction.)

Internal Credit Supports

With either a cash flow or market value structure a variety of "internal" credit supports may be used to help to increase the probability that investors will receive the level of returns promised. One common method is overcollateralization, in which additional assets are provided, such that their additional cash flow or market value are available to offset any losses stemming from defaults and delinquencies. For example, in a structure in which the cash flow from 100 mortgages is necessary to meet payments to security holders, the collateral pool might contain 110 mortgages, which would be sufficient to pay off security holders even if some of the mortgages defaulted.

One form of overcollateralization is a senior-subordinated structure, which divides the security into two or more classes, or tranches, with varying credit risk stemming from differences in their sequence of loss allocation. The risk of credit loss is thus shifted toward the lower-credit-quality (but presumably higher-yielding) tranches, while investors in the higher-credit-quality portions of the security are more cushioned against loss. As discussed in detail below, there is a complex array of internal credit supports (such as interest rate spreads) that can reduce the investor's risk of credit loss, typically by either adding collateral or by shifting risks among classes of security holders.

External ("Third-Party") Credit Supports

In addition to support from pledged assets, many structured financings include external credit support from a third party to the transaction, such as a bank or financial guarantor. The support generally takes the form of a corporate guarantee, a letter of credit (from a bank), an insurance policy, or a surety bond. If the third party provides unlimited ("full") credit support, the transaction is called a fully-supported structure. In "direct-pay" fully-supported structures, the third party is the primary source of payment. Alternatively, in "stand-by" fully-supported structures, the asset pool or underlying issuer is the first source of payment and the third party is the second source.

The same third-party credit supports may also be used to enhance the credit quality of conventional bonds, commercial paper programs, or other securities of companies as well as municipalities. The analysis of their value in enhancing credit quality is similar whether the supports are used to back an asset-backed financing or a conventional debt obligation of an issuer. Moody's approach to the analysis of third-party credit supports for either purpose is thus discussed under one heading below.

The Role of Ratings in the Structured Finance Market

Ratings serve a limited, but important, purpose in the structured finance market, as they do in the other markets that they cover. The ratings are opinions on the credit quality of the securities offered to investors, that is, the level of risk associated with the timely payment of principal and interest on a security over the life of the instrument. They are intended to serve as indicators of the relative risk premiums necessary to compensate investors for bearing the risk of credit loss.

As applied to particular structured finance issues or issuers, ratings are intended as indicators of the relative credit risk that investors may expect for securities rated at a given level. As in the rest of the corporate sector, ratings are forward-looking measures of a security's relative cushion (or level of protection) against credit loss under a variety of plausible scenarios, including both "best" and "worst" case situations that may occur over the life of the rated security. For long-term securities, "credit loss" refers both to the probability of default and to the relative magnitude of loss in the event of default; for short-term securities, only the risk of default is being measured.

As in the rest of the corporate sector, structured finance ratings are used by investors to evaluate whether or not a security meets their credit guidelines, to weigh the level of risk premium needed to offset credit losses, and for other credit-related decisions. In all cases, ratings are not intended to forecast protections against the other major investor concern, market risk (i.e., the risk the value of a security can change because of changes in interest rates, prepayment rates or the value of other call provisions, or foreign exchange rates). It should be noted, however, that ratings on particular structured securities may indirectly reflect market risk, but only to the extent that market risk of the assets backing the security will affect the risk of credit loss on the security itself.

To facilitate risk comparisons across all types of instruments, the same rating symbols are used to rate structured financings and all other types of debt obligations. For international consistency, Moody's sovereign rating ceilings are used to "cap" ratings on structured financings denominated in foreign currencies (i.e., currencies other than that of the issuer's country of domicile). Moreover, Moody's insurance, industrial, and bank letter of credit ratings are used consistently in rating decisions as indicators of the relative strength of all third-party credit supports provided by the same institution.

To further the consistency among ratings in all market sectors, Moody's often compares the "expected" credit loss on a particular structured issue with the credit losses that are consistent with Moody's rating categories. A structured security's expected loss is an average of the losses that the investor would experience under many alternative future scenarios, where each scenario is weighted by its probability of occurring. As noted earlier, for short-term securities, Moody's analyzes the expected default probability instead of the expected loss.

This rating approach has the virtues of being simple, yet comprehensive, and can be applied in a consistent manner across countries, security types, assets, and support mechanisms. Moreover, the system is consistent with that of the traditional corporate bond rating sector, which has a long-standing policy of considering the values added by the presence of collateral protection and/or senior payment position in assigning the debt rating of a corporate issue.

Although it is quantitative to some extent, credit analysis also relies heavily on judgment, requiring that ratings be provided by an independent, experienced organization. To that end, Moody's is a company that is independent of any government or financial institution, such as a commercial or investment bank. Its analysts have no direct involvement in the sale or trading of securities, instead focusing exclusively on credit analysis. Before turning to the many factors that are considered in Moody's credit analyses of the different types of structured securities, the next section presents a general description of the rating process.

The Rating Process for Structured Financings

In general, the process of researching credit fundamentals, reaching rating conclusions, and keeping market participants informed is the same for structured financings as for other segments of the credit markets. The entire rating process is scheduled to provide investors with timely rating information. However, unlike traditional unsecured obligations of a corporation, issuers of structured financings are typically in a position to "structure" appropriate investor credit protections to achieve a desired credit rating. Consequently, there may be many iterations of certain aspects of the rating process as issuers restructure the securities into their most profitable form. In addition, it is often possible for issuers to alter the structure over time to maintain a desired credit level as conditions change.

Developing a "Rating Approach" to Specific Types of Financings

Accordingly, the starting point in the rating process is to develop a generalized "rating approach" to particular types of financings. With asset-backed financings, that typically involves developing an understanding of the credit risk characteristics of particular asset types. The credit implications of typical legal and structural facets of the major types of financings are also studied. The information is often published in articles and special reports as part of Moody's Structured Finance service.

Initial Meetings with the Issuer

The rating approach is also useful as a framework for preliminary discussions between Moody's analysts and issuers who are in the process of structuring new securities. Typically, the meetings begin with a brief statement by the issuer's management, which may include an overview of the industry, the corporate strategy, and the purpose and structure of the security, followed by questions from Moody's analysts. A brief presentation of specific aspects of the security may follow: type of structure; collateral; credit supports; legal issues; and implications for the issuer's own credit risk, where appropriate.

Several members of Moody's senior management with direct involvement in the rating process are often present at the meeting. In addition, industry analysts from the "fundamental" areas of Moody's (i.e., the areas that rate the companies in the same industry) are often consulted. Subsequent discussion about the security and Moody's reaction to alternative structures that may be proposed are frequently conducted by telephone. In assigning ratings, Moody's often also works with the issuer's attorneys, investment bankers, and other participants in the transaction in a series of meetings beginning at the very early stages of the transaction. If the issue involves the sale of loans that are not government-guaranteed, Moody's analysts will normally visit the loan originators and servicers to examine underwriting and collection operations.

Rating Assignments

When the security's structure is nearly finalized, a "rating committee" meets to rate the security. The size and composition of the committee varies according to the special characteristics of the issue being rated. Commonly, the rating committee includes the lead analyst or analysts for the type of security being issued along with other Moody's analysts, and, possibly, managing directors with expertise applicable to the issue.

When a decision is reached, the issuer is informed. If changes to the structure are subsequently made, the rating committee generally meets again and informs the issuer about any effect on the rating. At the time of the closing, the issuer receives a letter stating Moody's rating and, where there is special market interest, the rating and a brief rationale are distributed to the relevant financial news media. A concise summary report on the issue and its main credit characteristics may also be published around the time of closing.

Credit Monitoring

Moody's analysts continuously monitor the credit quality of the assets backing each rated issue, looking specifically for rates of default or delinquency that are significantly above the range expected when the issue was originally rated. Data related to this collateral monitoring process are made available to investors in a variety of electronic and print formats. Analysts also maintain continuing surveillance for changes in the legal and regulatory environment, the quality of the servicer, etc. Changes in the credit quality of the issuer or of third-party providers of credit supports may also be a cause for a re-evaluation of the rating.

EVALUATING CREDIT RISK

Although the structured finance market covers a wide range of asset types and structures, each with its own set of special risks, those risks can generally be characterized as belonging to one of four general categories: asset risk, structural (cash flow) risk, legal risk, and third-party risk. *Asset risk* refers to the uncertainty concerning the extent to which the obligors of the underlying assets backing the security will pay as promised. The other three categories of risk refer to the degree to which the transaction is structured so that investors will receive payments as promised.

In this section we will outline the general credit quality issues that Moody's analyzes in each of those categories, as well as some of the major ways in which the analyses must be tailored to take into account the features of specific asset types and structures. The overriding goal, as mentioned earlier, is to provide a consistent analysis of credit risk across all structured financings and all Moody's ratings.

Asset Risks

General Framework
Analysis of the credit quality of any structured security that is backed by assets typically begins with an assessment of the risk in the underlying asset pool. Below we will discuss some of the methods Moody's uses in evaluating those asset pools, along with other asset considerations that may relate to the overall credit quality of the transaction.

Assets Can Supplement the Value of Third-Party Support An evaluation of the assets backing a transaction may be the logical starting point even if the transaction is fully supported by a third party. The assets generally enhance the value of a third party's support.

For a fully supported asset-backed security to default, the third party would have to default on its obligation and the funds from the assets would have to be insufficient to pay off investors as promised. Moreover, in the event of default, the severity of loss is likely to be lower, much as in the case of a traditional secured debt issue, since investors will receive funds from the assets in addition to any payments by the third party. Thus, depending on the quality of the assets and the correlation of that quality with the fortunes of the third party, the credit quality of a transaction that is backed by assets and fully supported by a third party can be higher than the credit quality of the third party itself.

Analogously, the credit quality could also be higher if, in addition to the full support of a third party, the transaction were backed by the promise of the firm raising the funds, instead of by assets. However, although the credit quality of assets and/or the issuer are important aspects of fully-supported transactions, the principal focus is the credit quality of the support provider and the legal structure of the support mechanism.[2]

Cash Flow versus Market Value Analysis The emphasis of collateral analysis is different depending on whether the transaction is based on a cash flow structure or a market value structure. With the former, the objective is twofold:

1. To assess the cash flows that investors will ultimately receive from the asset pool, which will depend on the portion of the pool that is ultimately charged off, and

---

[2] See the discussion of the credit support provider in the Third-Party Considerations section and the discussion of the third-party support mechanisms in the Legal and Regulatory Issues section later in this chapter.

2. To assess the timing of those cash flows, which is influenced by delinquency patterns, among other factors. The importance of timing in the
analysis depends on whether the instrument is short term or long term,
and on whether the structure allows for the accrual of interest that is
owed but not paid because of a shortfall of cash in a particular period.

In the case of market value structures, the focus is on the expected liquidation value of the assets should it be needed to pay off investor claims if the
issuer fails to do so. Market perceptions of the expected credit loss on the assets is
one factor that will affect that expected liquidation value; in addition, many other
factors must be considered, such as expected market liquidity, trends in interest
rates, and (for cross-currency issues) foreign exchange rates.

Incentive to Default and the Credit Quality of Obligors Moody's analysis
of the credit quality of an asset pool starts with an understanding of the key factors that affect the incentive and ability of obligors to pay off their loans as promised, and the magnitude of the loss if they do not. The incentive to continue
payments as promised depends on the net "benefit" to the obligor of, default. If
the net benefit is positive, then the obligor will choose to default, whether or not
the borrower has the ability to pay.

The net benefit consists of the present value of the monthly cash flows
that the obligor would avoid by defaulting, minus the costs of defaulting. Those
costs consist of both the value of the asset, if any, that would be repossessed in the
event of default, and other costs, such as the impact on the obligor's credit record,
the inconvenience of responding to dunning attempts by the creditor, deficiency
judgments (i.e., court-ordered payments by a borrower), bankruptcy costs, and the
general social attitudes toward, and ramifications of, default.

Moody's weighs the many factors that affect an obligor's incentive to
pay. The value of the remaining cash flows on the obligation depends on the original term to maturity and the rate at which the loan amortizes. The value of the
asset depends first, of course, on whether there is an asset (i.e., whether the loan is
secured), and then on how the asset appreciates or depreciates over time. Our
evaluation of the other costs of default depends on an understanding of the general social, institutional, and legal framework that influences defaults, which can
vary markedly across countries. However, even if the net benefit of defaulting is
negative, the borrower still may default if he or she does not have the ability to
pay and if the net value of the asset (i.e., the gross market value minus the cost of
disposing of it) is less than the remaining balance on the loan. Therefore, in addition to analyzing the net benefit of default to obligors, it is also important to evaluate the credit quality of the pool of obligors.

Because of the necessarily forward-looking nature of credit ratings,
Moody's analysis of those asset considerations does not simply rely on past data
and experience. Another element is essential: judgment regarding how the future
experience of the current pool can differ from the historical data. Portfolio data

are adjusted to account for recent trends, potential changes in overall regional or national economic performance, recent changes in the issuer's underwriting and collection procedures and policies, and any specific selection criteria used in the current pool that might cause its performance to differ from that of past portfolios.

Likely Loss Scenario and the Potential Variability of Loss Moody's overall assessment of each asset pool incorporates both (1) a determination of the most likely asset performance path and (2) a projection of the variability of that estimate, reflected in the many alternative scenarios that we examine in determining the expected (or, weighted average) loss on the security due to credit losses. For example, for cash flow structures, expected losses on the pool and the variability of those losses are weighed. For market value transactions, we would estimate the expected change in market value (including the impact of credit losses) and its variability.

Accounting for the potential variability of asset losses is important in the structured finance rating process because more variable pool losses, with constant expected pool losses, generally implies higher expected losses for investors. For example, suppose the expected loss was 3% of the original pool and the transaction had credit support that covered losses up to the first 5% of the original pool. Now, consider two stylized scenarios. First, assume that we knew the potential pool losses were not very variable. For example, suppose that at the most they could be 4% and, at the least, 2%, and that each of these outcomes had a 50% probability. Then, because of the 5% credit support, investors could never realize a loss; even at the maximum pool loss, the credit support would fully protect investors. Consequently, the credit quality of that security would be very high.

On the other hand, consider a more variable case, in which there was a 50% chance that losses could be 6% and a 50% chance that they would be 0%. Again, the expected pool loss is 3%. In that situation, however, if the maximum pool losses were realized, investors could suffer a loss of 1% (5% credit support minus 6% pool loss). Since, by assumption, we know this will occur with a 50% probability, the expected, or weighted average, loss to investors would be 0.5%. Therefore, as a result of the higher variability, the credit quality of that security would be lower.

The variability of potential pool loss outcomes can be reduced through diversification. Diversification lowers the chance that many of the assets in the pool will perform unfavorably at the same time. Pool diversification can be increased by increasing the number of assets in the pool, or by reducing concentrations in certain attributes, such as geographic location. The less correlated the performance of the assets, the greater the impact of diversification in lowering variability.

In the last section of this chapter, we will describe how Moody's analysts combine their estimates of the expected losses and variability with the credit support, if any, to determine both the expected yield loss attributable to credit losses and the rating. Now, however, we turn to describing some of the structural risks that Moody's evaluates in rating structured securities.

Structural Risks

The ultimate credit quality of a security depends not only on the riskiness of the asset or the borrowing firm, but also on the manner in which the transaction is structured to channel the benefits of the assets, payments from the borrower, or payments from other forms of support to investors.

Credit Support

As noted earlier, many types of credit enhancements can be used to increase the credit quality of a structured financing. Enhancement may be "external" to the security, in the form of an insurance policy, letter of credit, corporate guarantee, or surety bond. Those external enhancements can be used either in structures that are backed by assets or in those that have no asset backing but are fully supported by a third party. In addition, for asset-backed securities, the enhancement may be internal, as in the form of a "senior/subordinated" structure or interest rate spread in cash flow transactions, or overcollateralization in market value structures.

Moody's analysis of the credit support includes an evaluation of the initial size of the enhancement, how the size changes over time, and the conditions under which the enhancement is available to protect investors. In addition, for external forms of credit support, Moody's examines both the rating of the provider and the correlation of the credit strengths of the assets or the issuer/borrower with the entity providing the enhancement.[3]

Commingling

In many structures, funds owed to investors may be "commingled," or mixed together, with the funds of another party involved in the transaction. If that other party becomes insolvent or bankrupt, a bankruptcy court may find it difficult to determine the source and ownership of the commingled funds, so that investors may become unsecured creditors of the insolvent or bankrupt firm. For example, in many cash flow transactions, a servicer receives payments from obligors and is required to pass along a portion to investors. There is a lag, however, between the time funds are collected and paid. During this period, the funds may be commingled with the other funds of the servicer. If the servicer becomes bankrupt or insolvent, investors are at risk for the amount that has been paid to the servicer but not yet passed on to the investor. For servicers rated Prime-1, this risk is negligible. To reduce the risk with lower-rated servicers, the structure can provide for a separate account to receive funds on a daily basis for the benefit of investors, thus protecting against commingling. Alternatively, a letter of credit can be obtained from a third party to back up the servicer's payment obligation.

Similarly, in a fully-supported letter-of-credit structure, there may be the risk that payments made under the letter of credit will be commingled with payments by the borrower. That would increase the risk that would normally be associated with the funds from the generally high-credit-quality letter-of-credit provider.

---

[3] See the section on Third-Party Considerations.

Eligible Investments and Reinvestment Rates

During the period between the time the cash flow is received from the underlying assets or credit support providers of the security and the time it is paid to investors, the funds may be reinvested in financial assets. Moody's analysis examines the credit quality of the investments permitted within the structure, and the amount of reinvestment income that can be expected to be earned and available to investors.

Additional Structural Considerations for Asset-Backed Securities

Loss Allocation The quality of the support provided by assets depends not just on the credit quality of the asset pool itself, but also on the manner in which that support has been structured to be available to different investors. In some transactions, certain classes may have a position that is "senior" to other more "subordinate" classes with respect to losses. In a standard "senior/subordinated" structure, the senior and subordinated classes are backed by a common pool of assets. However, the subordinated class at any point in time absorbs the current losses on the entire pool (i.e., absorbs all chargeoffs) until it is exhausted; only if losses exceed the remaining subordinated principal balance would the senior class experience a loss. In effect, then, the subordinated class is backed by the "worst" portion of the pool (on an *ex post* basis), and the senior class by the "best."

The credit support provided by subordinated classes depends on the transaction's particular loss allocation method, of which there are many. For example, the senior class has less risk if it has a senior claim on both principal and interest payments, rather than on principal payments only.

Cash Flow Allocation A related point that Moody's evaluates in analyzing the credit quality of a multi-tranche structured financing is the payment priorities, or cash flow allocation, for principal and interest cash flows. In some securities, all principal and interest cash flows are initially paid to the "first" class; cash flow in excess of promised interest is used to pay down the balance of that class, while the unpaid interest to other classes accrues. That payment structure can reduce the risk to the first class, since the tranche's accelerated payment reduces exposure to future losses. Of course, any reduction in risk to the first class would be reflected in an increase in risk to another class.

Other cash flow allocation methods are also possible. For example, the first class may receive its pro rata share of principal, but the entire pool's interest payments. Or, it may be allocated only its pro rata share of interest and scheduled principal payments, but all of the prepayments from the pool. Alternatively, it may receive its pro rata interest share, but all of the pool's principal payments (i.e., scheduled payments and prepayments). In each case, the accelerated payments to the first class (vis-à-vis a completely pro rata cash flow allocation method) reduces the risk to the first class to some extent.

The reduction in risk to the first class, however, depends on the loss allocation method. The sharpest reduction occurs in structures in which losses are not allocated until there is a shortfall of cash flow at the end of the transaction, which may occur after the first class has been retired. Risk is reduced to a lesser extent if losses are allocated as they occur and if the allocation depends on original tranche balances instead of current balances.

A reserve fund structure is a somewhat different way of combining cash flow and loss allocation methods. In a reserve fund transaction, the senior tranche receives its pro rata share of interest and principal. However, the remaining principal inflows from the assets (or, principal and interest) are allocated to a reserve fund until it reaches a specified level, at which time excess payments can be paid to the subordinate class. Losses are paid from the reserve fund first and then from the cash flows owed to the subordinated tranche. Since some cash flows are "trapped" in the reserve fund to support the senior tranche, instead of being paid immediately to the subordinated class, the senior class in this senior/subordinated structure would be of higher credit quality than one in a structure that was equivalent except for the fact that the cash flows were allocated strictly on a pro rata basis.

Interest Rate Spread Interest rate spread refers to the difference between the interest earned on the assets and the sum of the (1) interest paid on the security and (2) servicing expenses. In some structures, this difference is available to serve as a cushion against losses, and consequently could lower the additional credit support that would be consistent with a particular rating level.[4]

Generally, interest spread is "worth more" (i.e., provides more effective support) if it is "trapped" in a "spread account" (instead of being distributed to the seller of the assets) and if unpaid pool losses are accrued instead of being taken immediately as a loss by the investor. Trapping the spread makes all past (unused) spread available to cover losses in a particular period; accruing the unpaid losses makes all future spread available to pay for those losses. For example, if losses are concentrated in one period, and if spread is not trapped and losses do not accrue, then the spread from that single period may not be sufficient to cover the (concentrated) losses. On the other hand, if the spread is trapped and losses accrue, the currently accumulated spread will, in general, cover more of the losses, and any future spread will be used to pay down at least some of the portion that was not previously covered.

Interest spread typically is not equal for all contracts in the pool. Therefore, in analyzing the credit-support value of interest rate spread to investors, Moody's adjusts the initial spread percentage for the possibility that "high spread" contracts might prepay before "low spread" contracts.

Changes in the Size of Credit Enhancement Over Time Credit enhancement levels generally decline as they are called upon to pay for losses. In addition, the dollar amount of credit support will also decline in some structures

---

[4] Similarly, in some structures the servicing fees are also available to pay for losses, providing additional enhancement.

because it is tied in some way to the amount of outstanding assets. For example, the dollar amounts of some letters of credit and surety bonds over time are a fixed percentage of the total outstanding pool contract balances, so that as the asset pool pays down, the dollar amount of support declines. Similarly, the credit support would decline in senior/subordinated structures in which the tranches received principal payments on a pro rata basis; in that case, the dollar amount of support provided to the senior class by the subordinated class would decline as the principal was repaid. And, in transactions in which the security receives at least some of its support from interest rate spread, the dollar amount of that support also would fall as the collateral is paid off.

For a given structure, obligor base, and credit enhancement level, allowing the credit support to decline over time weakens the structure of the transaction from the investor's perspective, all else being equal. Investor losses could be higher with declining credit support structures, especially if (1) prepayments are heavy early in the life of the transaction, causing the assets to pay down and the dollar amount of protection to decline, and then (2) heavy losses occur late in the life of the remaining contracts. This can be of particular concern because, with some types of assets, borrowers who prepay tend to be the higher-credit-quality obligors (such as loans for recreational vehicles and manufactured housing).

Modifying the Decline in Credit Enhancement Declines in credit support can be structurally modified in many ways. Declines that occur as the support is used to pay for losses can be "reinstated" by subsequent accumulations of interest rate spread. Declines in subordination levels can be mitigated by alternative cash flow allocation mechanisms, such as distributing all pool principal payments to the senior class until it has been fully paid off, as described earlier. And, instead of setting the enhancement level at a fixed percentage of the outstanding balances, the percentage can be scheduled to change over time, or can be specified in terms of a schedule of fixed dollar amounts.

Even in structures in which the credit enhancement generally is allowed to decline, other protections can be built into the transaction to limit the decline under special circumstances. For example, a "floor," or minimum dollar amount of credit support, can be specified; that is, the credit support generally would be allowed to decline as the contracts pay down, but would stop declining once it reached the floor, except to pay for subsequent losses. In addition, loss and/or delinquency "triggers" can be established; the credit support would only be allowed to decline if loss rates or delinquencies were below some specified levels, except to pay for losses. Another possibility is to allow less of a decline in credit support for prepaid principal than for scheduled principal repayments, thus offsetting to some extent the potential deterioration in pool credit quality that could arise from "adverse" prepayments (i.e., prepayments by obligors of higher average credit quality).

Wind-Down Events for "Revolving" Structures In some structures in which the assets are usually repaid relatively quickly, such as those backed by credit card or trade receivables, asset principal payments are normally reinvested in new receivables during an initial "revolving" period, instead of being paid to investors. After the revolving period, principal is paid to investors during the "amortization" period.

However, to protect investors against the possibility of a protracted period of deteriorating credit quality, revolving periods can be ended before their scheduled termination dates if certain "trigger" or "wind-down" events occur. Those wind-down events are generally designed to be "early warning" signals of declining credit quality, and the early termination of the revolving period is intended to reduce investors' exposure to losses that might develop as the asset quality continues to deteriorate. Typically, the events that can trigger a wind-down include declines in yield (i.e., finance charge payments and fees), payment rate, or new purchase rate, increases in losses or delinquencies, or the bankruptcy of the receivable originator. All else being equal, structures are of higher credit quality the "tighter" are the wind-down mechanisms (i.e., the less of a deterioration in credit quality necessary to trigger the wind-down).

Repurchase Provisions Another feature that can be incorporated into the structure to protect investors against losses is a repurchase, or "take-out," or "clean-up," provision. Typically, such a provision provides that a highly rated third party repurchase the remaining contracts in the pool at the end of some specified period or when the pool balance has fallen below some specified level, as long as the credit support is not exhausted. The transaction is therefore effectively ended for investors at that point, limiting their exposure to subsequent losses on the underlying pool. That is particularly important late in the life of the pool, when there may be only relatively few contracts remaining, leading to potentially highly variable subsequent pool performance. In general, for a particular structure, underlying pool, and credit enhancement level, the shorter the "take-out" or "call" period, the stronger the protection to investors.

Liquidity Facilities Liquidity facilities are important in structures in which the cash inflows may not match exactly the required payments to investors. The liquidity facility provides a temporary source of funds for cash flow that is ultimately expected from another source, in contrast to a credit support provider, which reimburses investors for shortfalls resulting from actual losses. The timing mismatches may result from delinquencies on the assets or from other unpredictable delays in asset payment, or, in the case of commercial paper programs, from an inability to sell new paper. Moody's analyzes the size of a structure's potential need for liquidity, the conditions under which the structure provides the liquidity, and the credit quality of the provider.

Legal and Regulatory Considerations

The main legal and regulatory considerations in structured financings are concerned with the potential insolvency of the issuer or other participants in the transaction. The issues that arise are generally those concerning whether the ownership of assets may be recharacterized by the courts or regulatory authorities and the extent to which legal or regulatory action can delay payment to investors.

Laws and regulations vary considerably from country to country, and sometimes across jurisdictions within a country. In many cases, the laws and regulations are developing with the evolving markets. For example, legislation in France created a legal structure (*fonds commune de creances*, or debt mutual funds) specifically for the issuance of asset-backed securities. In other countries, such as the United States, issuers typically have attempted to structure securities to fit into the body of law that existed before the development of the structured finance market, sometimes resulting in uncertainties regarding the way in which courts or regulators would apply the law to the relatively new market. The following is a description of some of the major legal and regulatory issues that arise in evaluating structured securities.

The Nature of Investors' Claims on the Assets

The extent to which investors will be able to realize the benefits of pledged assets depends on the way in which the rights in the assets were transferred. For example, in the United Kingdom, the rights can be transferred through either an equitable assignment or a legal assignment. The major difference is that in a legal assignment, the transfer is recorded and, in some regions, the issuer must notify borrowers of the transfer. The lack of notification in equitable assignments adds a number of risks to the transaction, including the possibility that the borrower may (legally) pay the originator instead of the issuer to whom the asset has been assigned. That would expose investors to the risk that the originator may become insolvent or fail to remit the funds to the issuer and could cause investors to suffer delays in payment or losses.

In the United States, a first-perfected security interest is somewhat analogous to the legal assignment in the United Kingdom. Essentially, the term "first" means that the investor has first priority on the assets. The "perfection" means that the claim has been properly registered to protect the interest. An unperfected security interest is somewhat analogous to the concept in the United Kingdom of equitable assignment. In addition, for transactions that are structured to include a reserve fund, investors can obtain a first-perfected security interest in the fund. In assessing the nature of investors' claims on the assets and reserve funds, Moody's often reviews legal opinions regarding the transfers of those claims.

Bankruptcy-Remote Issuers

Even when investors have a well-established claim in the assets, they are not assured of timely payment if the issuer of the security becomes the subject of an insolvency or bankruptcy proceeding. In that case, investors could be subject to a delay in exercising their rights with respect to the assets while a court sorts out the various claims. As a result, Moody's assesses the likelihood that the issuer will become insolvent or bankrupt. Factors that limit that likelihood include the following:

1. provisions that restrict the purpose of the issuer to that of issuing the securities,
2. provisions that restrict the ability of the issuer to incur additional debt or liabilities,
3. the ability of the issuer to pay for expenses out of capital and its revenue,
4. limitations on the issuer's ability to commence voluntary insolvency proceedings, and
5. limitations on the ability of other creditors to apply to the court system for relief.

"True Sale" of the Assets

In the United States, an investor's access to the benefits of the assets also may be impeded in the event of a bankruptcy filing by or against the seller of the assets. In that case, the court or regulator may rule that the assets were never sold, but merely pledged as collateral for a financing, and thus would possibly become subject to a court delay, or "stay." In addition, the court could allow the seller to substitute other collateral for the assets originally in the transaction. (In other countries, such as the United Kingdom, it is easier to legally establish the "sale" of an asset and hence the risk of delay or substitution is somewhat reduced.)

To determine whether the assets have been transferred in the form of a "true sale," or merely pledged, it is important to assess the extent to which the seller has retained an ownership interest in the assets. For example, Moody's examines the extent of recourse to the seller for defaulted assets, the subordinated interest and servicing fees retained by the seller, and the degree of control the seller has over the assets. In addition, a true sale opinion from a law firm may provide additional comfort that the transaction will be characterized as a transfer of assets rather than as a secured financing.

Substantive Consolidation

If the issuer is a subsidiary of a seller that becomes insolvent, a court may rule that their assets and liabilities must be consolidated in the insolvency proceeding, thereby again subjecting investors to the possibility of an insolvency-related delay. The following factors may mitigate that possibility:

1. the issuer retains a separate office at which it conducts its business,
2. the issuer has directors and executive officers who are not employees of the parent company,
3. the issuer's board of directors holds meetings to authorize all the issuer's corporate actions,

4. the issuer maintains separate corporate records and accounts,
5. the issuer's funds are not commingled with those of the parent,
6. the parent company acknowledges the separate existence of the issuer,
7. all corporate formalities are observed by the parent and the issuer,
8. the issuer is adequately capitalized in light of its business purpose and the transaction itself has a legitimate business purpose,
9. all business dealings between the parent and issuer are conducted on an "arm's-length" basis.

In addition, a legal opinion regarding substantive consolidation would add insight into the risk.

Principles of Fairness and Equity

While legal principles of fraud, fairness, and equity vary from country to country, many legal systems have some provisions for reversing transactions that are subsequently deemed to be unjust in some way. Those situations would typically arise in the event of an insolvency or a bankruptcy of the seller of assets. For example, if assets are deemed to have been sold for less than fair market value by an institution that becomes bankrupt or insolvent, a court may void the transaction, leaving investors with no collateral. In the United States, for example, such a sale could be challenged under applicable "fraudulent conveyance" laws. To protect against this risk, Moody's may use an opinion from a law firm that each transfer of assets is not fraudulent as evidence that the transfers will not be successfully challenged. In addition, Moody's will often examine statements by involved parties that a market price was paid for the assets.

In some countries, certain payments in a transaction also may be reversed if some creditors are deemed by a court to have been paid in a preferential way over other creditors while the payor was insolvent or bankrupt, or during some period immediately prior to insolvency or bankruptcy.[5] In that case, the recipient may be required to return the payment. Thus if an issuer of structured securities became insolvent, investors would be exposed to the risk of a forced return of funds already paid by the issuer.

For example, under United States bankruptcy laws, payments by an entity made while insolvent or within the applicable preference period immediately prior to a bankruptcy filing may be deemed preferential. There are a number of ways to mitigate that risk. First, as noted above, limiting the purpose and scope of activities of the issuer reduces the probability of issuer bankruptcy and therefore reduces the preference risk. Second, if the source of payment to investors is the cash flow from collateral, and if investors have a first-perfected security interest in the proceeds of the collateral, then preference risk is minimal. Third, such

---

[5] That preference period varies across jurisdictions. In the U. S., it is generally 90 or 123 days, depending on state bankruptcy laws and may be as long as one year in the case of payments to "insiders," as defined in the Bankruptcy Code.

entities as banks and thrifts are not subject to the bankruptcy code and therefore are not subject to the same preference risk. However, they are subject to regulatory authority to avoid (i.e., reverse) payments based on similar principles. Fourth, the structure could incorporate a third-party letter of credit expiring a sufficient number of days after the end of the transaction that could be drawn on to reimburse investors for any payments deemed preferential. Such a letter of credit is often referred to as a "clawback" letter of credit.

Fifth, bankruptcy laws provide that a payment will not be considered preferential if the payment is considered a contemporaneous exchange for new value or:

1. the debt was incurred by the issuer and the investor in the ordinary course of business of the issuer and investor,
2. the payment was made in the ordinary course of business of the issuer and investor, and
3. the payment was made according to ordinary business terms.

To conclude that these conditions were met, the following facts would have to be addressed:

1. the use of the proceeds of the debt,
2. the terms of the repayment to investors,
3. the sources of funds to repay investors,
4. the previous financing sources of the issuer, and
5. the type of investor purchasing the securities.

Application of the so-called "ordinary course" exception to the preference statutes is very sensitive to the particular set of circumstances, and therefore a legal opinion addressing all relevant facts may give Moody's greater comfort that this exception may be relied upon.

Sixth, the trustee could "age" the issuer's funds; that is, the trustee could hold the monies in a segregated account for a sufficient number of days before using the funds to pay investors. As a practical matter, this means that the issuer would have to make the first payment a sufficient number of days prior to the start of the transaction and continue to make advance payments throughout the term of the transaction to ensure that sufficient "aged" funds are always available to pay investors when due.

The preferential payment risk could arise in other contexts as well. For example, if a third-party provider of credit support were to become bankrupt, payments made under the support agreement during the applicable preference period prior to the bankruptcy could be deemed preferential and required to be returned, increasing the severity of the loss caused by the support-provider's bankruptcy.

Third-Party Support

In structures that provide for support by a third party, Moody's evaluates the type of support mechanism and its legal structure to determine the extent to which it allows the support to pass through to investors in an efficient and timely manner. As noted earlier, that is the major ingredient in the analysis of structures that are fully supported by third parties.

The main types of support mechanisms are letters of credit, corporate guarantees, parent company maintenance agreements, surety bonds, and irrevocable credit agreements. Of those, only letters of credit and surety bonds are generally independent of potential defenses by the support provider to avoid payments. Therefore, in evaluating the quality of the support mechanism, Moody's analyzes the extent to which those mechanisms have been specifically designed to limit the defenses to payment.

For example, with some corporate guarantees, the fiduciary is required to first look to the obligor for payment as a condition to collecting on the guarantee, possibly resulting in a delay in payment to investors. Similarly, unless the defense is specifically waived, providers of insurance policies and surety bonds may seek to avoid payment in the event of fraud or failure of consideration. In addition, irrevocable revolving credit agreements typically terminate immediately upon the insolvency of the issuer. That would significantly weaken the support unless the transaction is structured to make the issuer insolvency-remote. Therefore, those agreements tend to be used in structures in which the liquidity but not the insolvency of the issuer is a concern.

Moody's evaluates a number of other risks when the credit support is between affiliated parties, such as in a parent company guarantee or maintenance agreement. Parent guarantees may be deemed unenforceable for a number of reasons, including the absence of an "arm's length" relationship between the parent and the subsidiary. There is also the possibility that the holders, as only indirect beneficiaries of the support, may not be entitled to bring enforcement action. Moreover, there is the risk that payments under the guarantee might be recharacterized by the court or regulatory authority as funds of the issuer and frozen or delayed in the event of the issuer's bankruptcy.

Enforceability and timeliness of payment are also key factors in the analysis of parent company maintenance agreements. Those agreements may be considered executory contracts (i.e., contracts under which the obligations have yet to be performed) by the courts and therefore may not be enforceable in the event of a bankruptcy of the parent or the subsidiary. With respect to timely payment, funds paid from the parent to the subsidiary under the agreement may get trapped in the bankruptcy proceedings of the subsidiary. Another factor that Moody's considers is the cost to the parent of not supporting the subsidiary, which depends on the strategic and financial importance of the subsidiary to the success of the parent and the costs of abrogating an obligation, in terms of damage to the parent's reputation, market access, and business position.

The most fundamental risk for a letter of credit is whether it is drawn as an irrevocable and unconditional obligation of the bank. Moody's analyzes the extent to which the bank may be able to cancel or otherwise avoid its payment obligations.

Consumer Protection Laws

Consumer protection laws can also have an impact on the riskiness of structured securities. In the United Kingdom, for instance, violation of consumer protection laws that apply to consumer debt may make the debt unenforceable. For example, provisions of the Consumer Credit Act of 1974 that apply to loans of less than £15,001 provide for licensing of, and other controls on, participants in the credit-granting process. If those provisions are violated, the loans may be unenforceable.

Regulatory Considerations

For regulated institutions, such as banks and thrifts in the United States, Moody's analyzes the transaction under the regulations of the agency that would become the receiver for a failed institution (e. g., the Federal Deposit Insurance Corporation). Of particular interest, of course, is whether the structures would maintain their integrity upon receivership. Moody's bases its interpretation of likely regulatory response on many factors, among which are verbal discussions with, and/or written assurances from, the appropriate agency and how a court would view the situation.

Evaluating the Credit Quality of Third Parties

The Servicer

In structured finance transactions the issuer often has no employees or facilities and hence must retain a third party, the servicer, to administer the day-to-day operations of the transaction. Those operations include routine asset portfolio administration duties, such as determining interest rates on assets, managing the flow of payments from borrower to issuer, and collecting late payments. Other responsibilities may include advancing funds to provide liquidity to cover loans in arrears, overseeing activities of sub-servicers, and temporarily reinvesting idle cash in short-term investments.

The impact of poor performance, or temporary nonperformance, of the servicing function obviously depends on the servicer's role in the transaction. If the servicer advances funds, for example, alternative sources of liquidity need to be evaluated. Furthermore, in transactions that are backed by the liabilities of lower-credit-quality obligors, which require active collection efforts, a decline in the quality, or a temporary suspension, of the collection effort may lead to a rise in delinquencies and losses. In addition, if a servicer becomes insolvent, funds flowing through the servicer could be tied up in insolvency proceedings; moreover, a liquidator or receiver could use provisions of the bankruptcy or insolvency laws to require the issuer to return sums that were previously paid by the servicer to the issuer.

To assess the likelihood that the servicing functions will be performed satisfactorily throughout the term of the transaction so that investors are paid on a timely basis, Moody's considers the credit quality of the servicer, whether the structure provides for a backup servicer in the event of the primary servicer's insolvency, and the ease with which a substitute servicer could be found, if necessary. The ease with which a backup servicer can be found depends on several key factors, as follows:

1. the complexity of the servicer's role in the transaction,
2. the depth of the secondary market for servicing,
3. the existence of consumer protection laws that might restrict the ready transfer of servicing rights,
4. the performance of the pool and hence the cost of servicing it, and
5. the amount of servicing fees provided for in the transaction.

The Credit Support Provider

In structures that have external forms of credit or liquidity support, the credit quality of the structure is at least partially dependent on the credit quality of the support provider. That dependence is most pronounced for structures that are fully supported by a third party. However, that does not necessarily make third party-supported structures "riskier" than structures that are fully supported internally, such as senior/subordinated transactions. In internally supported structures, the analogous risk is that of a decline in the credit quality of the assets supporting the senior class. Externally supported structures simply substitute the credit quality of the third party for at least some of the support provided internally.

When third-party support is only partial — that is, when the structure is supported partly by assets and partly by the third party — the structure's rating depends on both the size of the enhancement and the rating of the provider. To some extent, more credit support can compensate for a lower rating on a credit support provider. That is because Moody's approach is to weight all kinds of future scenarios in determining a rating. There are some future scenarios in which a lower-quality provider would not fulfill its obligations, leading to some investor losses. However, there are also other possible scenarios in which a higher-quality provider, furnishing less support, would not cover all pool losses, which would also lead to investor losses. Therefore, the average reduction in investor losses could be the same under the two support structures, making them equivalent from a credit analysis perspective.

Furthermore, for structures that depend on the credit quality of an asset pool or the issuer/borrower, as well as the credit quality of the credit enhancement provider, a downgrade of the provider will not necessarily lead to an equivalent downgrade of the structured financing. Whether the structure is downgraded, and the extent of any downgrade, depends on the (1) extent of the downgrade of the provider of the credit support, (2) amount of support provided, (3) performance of the pool or borrower, and (4) paydown of various classes (for asset-backed securities).

In rating a structured transaction, Moody's also looks at the correlation of the credit strengths of the asset pool and of the entity providing enhancement. The less the correlation, the stronger is the degree of protection provided by a given level of credit support. For example, the performance of a foreign bank supplying credit support may not be highly correlated with the credit risk of a pool of U. S. mortgages. If the foreign bank is downgraded, the performance of the assets may not have declined as much, partially offsetting the lower quality of the guarantee. On the other hand, if the two are highly correlated, the support provider may not be in a position to fulfill its obligation exactly in those circumstances in which it will be needed, leading to greater exposure to possible losses.

Other Third Parties

There are a number of other important third parties that provide various commitments and services to a structured transaction, all of which can affect the timely and ultimate payment of principal and interest to security holders. Some of those third parties and a sample of their commitments are the following:

> *Guaranteed Investment Contract Provider* — Insures reinvestment rate on investable funds.
>
> *Paying Agent* — Pays principal and interest to security holders; may collect and hold funds prior to distribution.
>
> *Trustee* — Processes payments to security holders, enforces indenture, often provides backup to other third parties, such as Master Servicer.
>
> *Investment Banker* — Provides fair value representations.
>
> *Accountants* — Provide auditing checks.
>
> *Issuer's Counsel* — Provides legal opinions on security interests, ownership interests, and bankruptcy issues.
>
> *Depository* — Makes payment to security holders, controls issuance of commercial paper.

To assess the impact of a third-party commitment on the risk of a structured transaction, Moody's follows a two-step process. First, Moody's assesses the likelihood that the third party will not fulfill its commitment or may perform it incorrectly. Second, the consequences of an incomplete performance of the commitment are weighed and quantified to the extent possible. To assess the risk of nonperformance by the third party in carrying out its required responsibilities and commitments, Moody's looks at its credit quality, operational experience, and level of expertise.

PUTTING ALL THE PIECES TOGETHER — THE RATING JUDGMENT

As outlined in this chapter, the credit performance of a structured security depends on myriad factors, including the performance of the assets or primary obligor; the extent to which third parties fulfill their obligations; the legal risks; and the structure's flow of funds, which determines the conditions under which third parties would be called upon and allocates the cash flows from the assets and third parties to investors.

In determining a rating, Moody's analyzes a wide range of possible economic and legal scenarios that would determine the amount of cash that would flow into the structure, and assigns a probability to each scenario, depending on the variability of, and correlation among, the various inputs. Then, given the flow of funds structure of the transaction, we analyze the cash flows that investors would ultimately receive under each scenario, and determine whether the payment promises to investors would be kept. As noted earlier, that determination is somewhat different for short- and long-term ratings; for short-term ratings, we simply look at the probability that the promises will not be fulfilled, while for long-term ratings, we also account for the magnitude of any shortfall that might occur.

It is often asserted that ratings represent the ability of a security to "withstand" a "worst case" scenario; for example, a security rated Aaa will withstand a depression and a security rated Aa will withstand a severe recession. Alternatively, a "worst case" may be determined as a multiple of expected losses on an asset pool. However, because Moody's long-term ratings take into account not only the probability of loss but also the severity, that "worst case"-type analysis is, at best, only a rough approximation of our general approach. Two structured financings that perform similarly in a "worst-case" scenario may perform very differently under even slightly altered circumstances. Therefore, "worst-case" performance provides only limited information regarding the overall credit quality of the instrument.

Thus our rating judgment relies on an analysis of multiple future scenarios. While those scenarios sometimes may be based on quantitative models such as regression analysis or Monte Carlo simulations, they nevertheless also depend to a great extent on the judgment of analysts. The asset pool that is currently being analyzed rarely, if ever, has exactly the same characteristics as the assets from which the historical data have been generated. In addition, the current economic and legal environment can also be quite different than that of the past. Consequently, the rating of structured securities requires a blend of quantitative analysis and experienced judgment.

Chapter 6

The Role of Financial Guarantees in Asset-Backed Securities

Mahesh K. Kotecha
Managing Director
MBIA and CapMAC Asia

INTRODUCTION

One of the key reasons behind the rapid expansion of the asset-backed securities (ABS) market in the United States since it began in the mid-1980s has been the widespread availability and acceptance of third-party credit enhancement. With the application of financial guarantees, historically a mainstay of the municipal bond industry, and other sources of credit enhancement, ABS have come to be viewed as safe, liquid, and high-yielding investments. Institutional investors appreciate the fact that a financial guarantee company has analyzed the complex structure of an asset-backed issue and can provide an assurance that all interest and principal payments will be made on time and in full. And they know that since the financial guarantee industry was founded in 1971, over $1 trillion of debt has been guaranteed by the industry, with no defaults by any guarantors on any guaranteed obligation. Industry-wide acceptance of third-party credit enhancement has meant that an increasing number of issuers are enjoying the many benefits of financial guarantees, which include a reduced cost of funds, longer tenors, a wider investor base, and access to capital markets that might otherwise prove difficult or expensive. It has also helped make ABS as important a financing alternative as equities, bonds, or bank loans.

The discussion in this chapter of the role of financial guarantees in ABS is based on extensive experience in dealing with issuers and their concerns regarding credit enhancement and financial guarantees, in particular. The chapter examines fundamental aspects of the financial guarantee industry so that issuers and investors can both appreciate the dynamics of the business and better utilize this credit enhancement alternative. The issues addressed include: the benefits of financial guarantees, regulatory and rating agency concerns, applying a financial

Research and editorial assistance for this chapter was provided by Bill Martens, an associate at MBIA.

guarantee, the surveillance process, fees, market spreads, etc. In short, this chapter provides a framework to help issuers understand and deal with financial guarantors.

CREDIT ENHANCEMENT ALTERNATIVES

Various credit enhancement structures have been used for ABS, including senior/subordination, cash collateral or collateral investment accounts, and third-party support from bank letters of credit or financial guarantees. Issuers need to understand the benefits and costs of the credit enhancement options available to them.

Letters of Credit

The oldest form of credit enhancement is the *letter of credit* (LOC) from a top-rated international bank. LOCs were generally provided on a "partial" basis — that is, coverage of credit losses on the underlying asset pool that was less than 100% of the pool but enough to gain a triple-A rating. The popularity of this form of enhancement has waned because few banks have retained triple-A ratings from both Standard & Poor's and Moody's Investors Service, not to mention "event" risk associated with LOCs. In addition, new regulations have made the business of providing LOCs for ABS transactions considerably less appealing for banks. As a result, LOCs have become more expensive, less beneficial, and less available. This is one reason why the market has increased its reliance on the three other credit enhancement techniques.

Senior/Subordination

Senior/subordination, which involves over-collateralization, is a form of credit enhancement internal to the transaction. In reality it is a form of "investor segmentation" through which credit risk is split between different classes of investors with different risk appetites.

In its basic form, a senior/subordinated structure has two parts:

1. An "A" or senior tranche, which represents the majority of the asset pool. This piece is rated triple-A, or sometimes double-A, and sold to investors seeking to limit credit and duration risk.
2. A "B" or subordinated tranche, which is junior in payment priority to the "A" tranche and designed to bear losses on the entire pool. It usually has a longer maturity, more uncertain duration and lower credit rating. Consequently, "B" tranche investors are paid a market premium for the extra risk.

Subordinated tranches may be further credit-enhanced with letters of credit, cash reserves against first losses, and partial or 100% surety bonds issued by a financial guarantor.

Senior/subordinated structures can limit the need for third-party credit enhancement, premiums for which are replaced in effect by a higher return paid on the "B" tranche. For some well-accepted asset classes, senior/subordinated structures have become the norm. However, for newer asset classes or complex transactions or longer-dated collateral types, market participants continue to find financial guarantees and other forms of third-party credit enhancement useful, both in attracting investors and completing the deal.

Cash Collateral Accounts and Collateral Investment Accounts

A technique of recent vintage is the *cash collateral account* (CCA). While the LOC business has largely been the domain of triple-A rated institutions, lower rated lenders can also provide third-party credit enhancement via cash collateral accounts. Initially developed to support ABS backed by credit card receivables, these accounts provide a reserve of cash, which is designed to bear the credit and liquidity risks of a transaction.

In practice, a loan is made to a special purpose entity (a corporation, trust or limited partnership, sometimes called a *special purpose vehicle* or SPV) which has been set up to issue the securities. As long as the bank has a short-term rating of A-1/P-1 or higher, the vehicle company redeposits the loan back with the lending bank. As with a LOC, the bank receives a fee, which, in this case, is the difference between the interest rate paid by the SPV to the bank on the loan and the interest rate paid to the SPV by the bank on the deposit. While both rates are often set with reference to LIBOR, the fee can end up being a fixed spread of ½% to 1%.

The cash collateral account has evolved fairly quickly into the *collateral investment account* (CIA), effectively replacing both the LOC and CCA. With the CIA, the lender of the CCA is replaced with an investor who purchases a subordinated certificate from the issuer. While the lender of the CCA and the investor in the CIA are in effect taking the same risks, the CIA method permits the seller/servicer to remove more receivables from its balance sheet, increasing the efficiency of the transaction. While any investor could, in principle, purchase the subordinated certificate, the former LOC and CCA banks continue to dominate as providers of the CIA as they are typically familiar with the business and have liquid balance sheets, though the recent spate of big bank mergers could change the mix of participants.

The CCA and CIA techniques have become popular, particularly for commodity-type, consumer-receivables backed transactions. The providers have typically been the lenders that had been active in providing LOCs. This is not surprising, since the lender must:

- have or develop the expertise to assess the creditworthiness of the borrower, the collateral, and the ABS structure.
- be willing to balloon the institution's balance sheet by making the loan, and thus restrict its ability to deploy its capital more profitably elsewhere.

- in the case of CIAs, be willing to assume a funding risk in the event its rating drops below A-l/P-I and the SPV moves its cash deposit to another institution. In this event, the issuer may have to pay a higher rate on the loan if the loan conditions permit the lender to pass along a part or all of its higher funding costs.

FINANCIAL GUARANTEES DEFINED

A financial guarantee (sometimes referred to as *bond insurance* or a *surety bond*) is used in ABS transactions to enhance a security to the high investment grade level based on the financial guarantee company's rating. The guarantee is designed to ensure that investors receive timely payments of principal and interest (without acceleration, except at the option of the guarantor), regardless of whether the underlying collateral assets are able to support such payments.

The financial guarantee law of New York state defines a financial guarantee narrowly as "a surety bond, insurance policy, or ... an indemnity contract ... under which loss is payable upon proof of occurrence of financial loss, to an insured claimant, obligee, or indemnitee ... as a result of a failure of an obligor to perform under a payment obligation as a result of a default or an insolvency." Under this law, financial guarantee companies are permitted to underwrite credit risk but not market risk (the risk of changes in prices of collateral assets). However, they may enhance transactions where the market risk is in fact remote but where the credit risk is related to the market value of the underlying collateral. One example is the so-called market value (as distinct from cash flow) collateralized bond obligation or CBO. Some of these securities are backed by a pool of corporate bonds, the market value of which must be maintained at an agreed multiple of senior securities using a pledge of additional collateral. If the issuer fails to meet this mark-to-market obligation, the trustee is authorized to sell a part of the pool of bonds until the agreed multiple is restored.

Financial guarantees are used to support principal and interest payments for a wide range of obligations. Financial guarantee companies have partially or fully insured financings backed by cash flows or market values of assets held not only in the United States but also in other industrialized and emerging market countries. Guaranteed transactions involve such collateral assets as first mortgages, home equity loans or second mortgages, major bank and private label credit card balances, auto loans and leases, boat loans, recreational vehicle loans, manufactured housing loans, timeshare vacation apartment loans, perpetual floating-rate notes, high yield bonds, senior loans to highly leveraged companies, commercial real estate leases, municipal leases, etc.

It is important to note that the term "financial guarantee" as defined here is distinct from the European term, which also includes "credit insurance," the practice whereby an insurance company may indemnify merchants extending credit to customers against loss or damage resulting from non-payment of loans.

THE BENEFITS OF FINANCIAL GUARANTEES

Issuers have found that financial guarantors are willing to consider innovative transactions in new markets, involving new classes of assets or novel structures or longer maturities. Financial guarantors are typically able to deal with longer-term asset classes, such as home equity loans and manufactured housing, which bank providers of credit enhancement are less willing to consider. Issuers have also benefitted from the widespread acceptance of financial guarantees among investors as this makes deals more marketable.

An issuer concerned only with a sale under generally accepted accounting principles (GAAP) or window dressing may prefer senior subordination or over-collateralization since the recourse it provides to senior investors by retaining a part or all of the subordinated piece still permits off-balance sheet treatment while minimizing direct expenses. On the other hand, third-party credit enhancement permits regulatory accounting sale as regulators are typically concerned about the level of recourse, including the "moral hazard." Third-party credit enhancement can also maximize receivables utilization by increasing proceeds of the securitization for the seller/servicer. Finally, it also transfers catastrophic credit risk to the bank or financial guarantor providing a full guarantee.

For a number of reasons, investors also increasingly value the benefits of financial guarantees. First, the investor can be confident that the transaction structure is inherently safe and will likely remain so. Since financial guarantors are placing their own rating and capital on the line with each transaction, it is in their interest not only to impose stringent conditions at the outset, but also to continue to monitor credit and asset pool quality. Second, the investor also benefits from the oversight of the rating agencies on both the transaction and the financial guarantee company. Each guaranteed transaction must in general be reviewed, approved, and deemed investment grade in its own right by the rating agencies. Third, financial guarantees enable the underwriter to simplify distribution of ABS to investors, thereby improving the liquidity and the economics of the transaction. ABS which do not include third-party credit enhancement often require the investor to have a more thorough understanding of the underlying transaction structure, and the specific collateral backing the issue. The benfits of financial guarantees from the perspective of issuers and investors are summarized in Exhibit 1.

Issuers and investors have both developed a high level of confidence in financial guarantees in part because of the industry's unusual performance record. Unlike LOC banks, no U.S. financial guarantee company has suffered a rating downgrade in the 27-year history of the industry. Furthermore, no investor in any guaranteed security has missed a single timely payment of principal or interest.

Exhibit 1: Benefits of Financial Guarantees

Issuers	Investors
Higher ratings	Investment grade ratings
Easier capital markets access	Guaranteed timely payments
Broader investor base	Higher liquidity
Longer maturities	Superior yield with limited risk
Financing flexibility	Matched assets and liabilities
Lower borrowing costs	Experienced risk assessment
Liability management	Monthly, proactive surveillance
Less public disclosure	

Exhibit 2: Financial Guarantors and their Ratings

Financial Guarantor	Claims Paying Ability Rating			
	S&P	Moody's	Fitch IBCA	Duff & Phelps
MBIA	AAA	Aaa	AAA	NR
AMBAC	AAA	Aaa	AAA	NR
FGIC	AAA	Aaa	AAA	NR
FSA	AAA	Aaa	AAA	NR
Axa Re Finance	AAA	NR	AAA	NR
Capital Reinsurance	AAA	Aaa	AAA	NR
Enhance Reinsurance	AAA	Aaa	NR	AAA
Asset Guarantee Insurance	AA	NR	NR	AAA
American Capital Access	A	NR	A	A
Commercial Guaranty Assurance	A	NR	NR	AAA
ASIA Ltd.	BB	NR	NR	A

FINANCIAL GUARANTORS

Financial guarantors are sometimes referred to as "monoline" insurance companies because they engage in mainly one line of insurance business, namely, financial guarantees. This is in contrast to "multiline" insurance companies, which engage in a variety of other lines of business, including but not limited to life insurance, annuities, accident and health insurance, fire insurance, miscellaneous property insurance, personal injury or property damage liability insurance, fidelity insurance, residual value insurance, etc. Regulatory restrictions do not permit multilines licensed in New York and certain other states to provide financial guarantees, except through separately capitalized subsidiaries. While some non-U.S. property and casualty insurers with top ratings have acted as reinsurers or insurers for ABS, they have generally done so with caution. We have focused mainly on triple-A rated, monoline financial guarantee companies, most of which are based in the United States.

As of early 1998, there are 11 providers of financial guarantees which act as primary insurers or as reinsurers specializing in various aspects of the business. The ratings of these 11 providers are reported in Exhibit 2. The market is domi-

nated by four companies, all of which guarantee both the borrowings of municipalities, states and other non-Federal government entities, and structured
financings. They are: AMBAC Indemnity Corporation (AMBAC); Financial
Guaranty Insurance Company (FGIC); Financial Security Assurance Inc. (FSA);
and Municipal Bond Investors Assurance Corp. (MBIA). The share of each of
these providers in 1997 is shown in Exhibit 3. As a practical matter, this has
evolved into a primarily triple-A claims paying ability ratings market, though
there are now some niche market guarantors with lower ratings.

The seven other financial guarantors are essentially niche players. The
two major reinsurers within the industry, each with a small direct insurance
capacity, are Capital Reinsurance Company (Cap Re) and Enhance Reinsurance
Company (Enhance Re). Asset Guaranty Insurance, an affiliate of Enhance Re,
has a claims paying ability rating of AA and does only about a third of its business in the primary insurance market. It was formed to undertake the smaller or
more complex transactions and to provide Enhance Re with additional capacity
for single risks. Axa Re Finance was formed in 1996 by Axa Reinsurance S.A. as
a means of taking a more focused approach toward the financial guarantee and
reinsurance businesses.

Two other specialized guarantors entered the industry in 1997 intending
to focus on niche markets which had not been well-served before. With a claims
paying ability rating of A, American Capital Access concentrates on lower rated
and unrated issuers in a variety of markets. Commercial Guaranty Assurance,
which also holds a claims paying ability rating of A, provides credit enhancement
primarily to the commercial real estate-backed and private asset-backed markets,
where existing guarantors have participated to a lesser extent.

Historically, there has been a clear delineation between guarantors focusing on the municipal and ABS markets in the United States. These distinctions
have blurred over the past several years as guarantors have diversified and competition in the industry has increased. These trends have been driven by slower
growth in the municipal market, rapid expansion of the ABS market, and an
increased emphasis on building market share in Europe and Asia. Guarantors have
also widened the range of their credit enhancement and other related activities.

Exhibit 3: Public Asset-Backed Market (% Share, 1997)

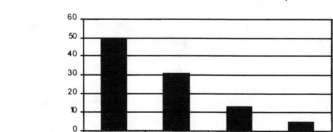

There has been significant consolidation within the financial guarantee industry since 1997. After completing its privatization from the federal government early in the year, specialty guarantor Connie Lee, which had focused on the health care and education sectors, was purchased by AMBAC in late October. Also, AMBAC Financial Group purchased Cadre Financial Services, an investment advisor; MBIA purchased a 95% stake in Municipal Tax Bureau, a financial services company; and, Enhance Financial Services acquired the outstanding shares of Singer Asset Finance, a securitization company. And in February 1998, industry leader MBIA and CapMAC merged, expanding their capabilities in structured finance and international markets.

With the emergence of an international ABS market, financial guarantee companies have also become more active abroad, guaranteeing transactions in Argentina, Australia, France, Hong Kong, Italy, Indonesia, Mexico, New Zealand, Spain, Thailand, and the United Kingdom. FSA, FGIC, AMBAC, and Cap Re have all opened overseas offices. And MBIA Assurance S.A. and Financial Security Assurance (UK) Ltd have set up Paris and London-based affiliates to concentrate on the European market. In addition, AMBAC and MBIA formed a joint venture in 1995 to take advantage of business opportunities outside the US.

Last but not least, ASIA Ltd was formed in December 1995 by CapMAC, Asian Development Bank, Government of Singapore Investment Corporation, Malaysian Employee Provident Fund, and a number of other investors to focus on Asian infrastructure and asset backed securities. Reflecting the rating downgrades in Asia since mid-1997, ASIA Ltd was downgraded by S&P from A to BB and by Duff & Phelps from AA to A, in what were the first downgrades of a financial guarantor. As of this writing, the company had not suffered any credit loss or paid any claims as its guarantee portfolio had continued to perform well and was working on a recapitalization plan to double its claims paying resources and regain its original ratings.

The recent economic crisis in Asia has led to increased credit concerns on the part of international investors and lenders. Economic and financing activity in the region will no doubt slow for the next couple of years, but if the adjustment programs undertaken with the IMF are generally successful, growth will likely resume in the medium term. Though the potential securitization market in Asia is now limited to offshore receivables and some local currency securitizations, a number of favorable factors loom ahead which might improve its viability: market spreads have widened, financial sectors are being restructured and recapitalized, and many countries are initiating capital market and regulatory reforms. While Asia's financing needs may remain only partially met in the near term, latent demand for funding over the next decade remains enormous — perhaps in excess of US$1.5 trillion. As and when investor confidence returns and the demand for securitization grows, financial guarantors are likely to play a vital role in providing access to capital markets.

REGULATORY AND RATING AGENCY CONTROLS ON FINANCIAL GUARANTORS

Regulatory and rating agency oversight on financial guarantors has fostered investor confidence and facilitated an expanding role for financial guarantees in the ABS market. A number of states, including New York, Florida, California, Illinois, Connecticut, Iowa, New Jersey, and Wisconsin, currently have specific insurance laws regulating financial guarantee companies. As an example, the New York statute establishes:

- single risk limits applicable to all obligations tailored to the various types of obligations guaranteed, to ensure that no single risk is disproportionate to the capital of the guarantor.
- aggregate risk limitations, also tailored to the various types of obligations guaranteed, to ensure that the aggregate book of business is not disproportionate to its capital.
- contingency reserve requirements, to ensure that the company sets aside reserves with respect to each obligation guaranteed and, effectively, increases its capital base over time.
- case basis loss reserves, i.e., reserves against actual defaults on guaranteed transactions, and unearned premium reserves to protect the company against losses.

Insurance regulations in effect dictate the amount of capital a guarantor must maintain to support its book of business. The capital required takes into account the different features of the various guaranteed transactions and is based on predetermined leverage ratios for individual categories. In addition, each financial guarantee company must also comply with the insurance regulations of all states in which it is licensed to do business. From state to state, regulations restrict such operations as investments of capital and surplus funds, as well as payments of dividends.

Financial guarantee companies are also reviewed on an ongoing basis by the credit rating agencies. In assigning a triple-A or other high investment grade rating, the rating agencies must be satisfied that the financial guarantee company has sufficient capital to meet its guaranteed obligations on a timely basis, under a variety of economic and financial scenarios called "stress tests," including a simulation of the Great Depression. The agencies periodically review the company's management and business plan, its shareholder group, underwriting standards and procedures, diversification of guaranteed portfolio risks, monitoring procedures, exposure limits, and capital adequacy. Analysts from the rating agencies also review each company's financial performance, including the performance of its investment portfolio.

Furthermore, the agencies must satisfy themselves that each guaranteed transaction meets investment grade standards. Rating agencies assign a "capital charge" for each transaction (defined later) and make sure that the company has sufficient capital to support the aggregate book of business.

Each of the financial guarantee companies, regardless of its ownership structure, is also subject to an annual audit by an independent certified public accounting firm.

THE PROCESS OF UNDERTAKING A FINANCIAL GUARANTEE

An ABS issuer or client seeking a financial guarantee — a banker, broker or seller of assets — typically initiates the process with an inquiry to a potential provider of the coverage. At this stage, the issuer has usually decided that the transaction requires credit enhancement from a third party. The guarantor screens the inquiry to determine whether the proposed ABS transaction measures up to its own business strategy, underwriting standards, reinsurance capacity, risk diversification objectives, and return targets. If the proposed transaction meets these requirements, the guarantor then indicates interest and specifies its premium and structural requirements. The client of the guarantor either accepts the preliminary terms or seeks an alternative form or source of credit enhancement.

The issuer may select its credit enhancement technique in conjunction with its investment banker and/or its financial advisor (if any). For commodity-type deals, the issuer may conduct what is in effect an auction. In other cases, the issuer may choose to work with a particular financial guarantor because of its reputation, prior experience and expertise, pricing and trading value, structural requirements, and ability to deliver on a timely basis.

Next, the guarantor carries out its "due diligence" on the transaction, to enable it to reach its risk underwriting decisions. This investigation involves three basic steps:

1. the legal risks of the ABS transaction are assessed, to ensure that cash flows to investors would be unimpeded by bankruptcy of the seller/servicer, typically through a "true sale" to a bankruptcy remote special purpose vehicle.
2. the seller/servicer is assessed, not only to determine its general creditworthiness, but also its ongoing ability to originate and service the assets being pooled in the transaction and the need for a "back up" servicer.
3. the guarantor assesses cash flow risks by simulating several "worst case" scenarios and evaluating their impact on the structure and the cash flows of the ABS in question. The simulations are typically carried out through appropriate quantitative models (e.g. the Monte Carlo technique or simple cash flow models) to test the structure's response to high levels of unemployment, rising interest rates and other adverse conditions.

Exhibit 4: First and Second Loss Protection

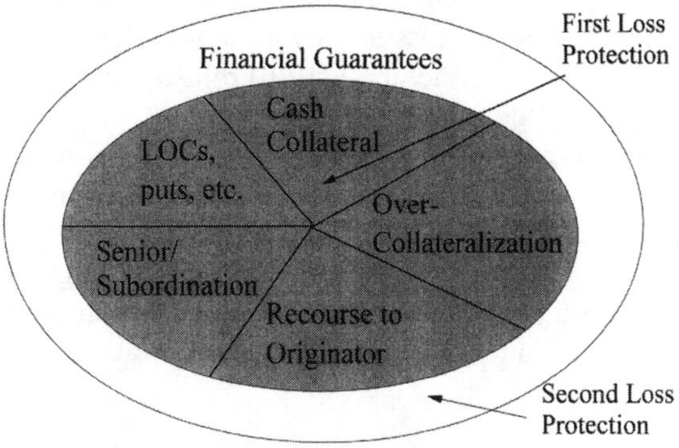

The object of the exercise is to create a balanced structure meeting the needs of the seller/servicer and investors, assuring the investor and the guarantor that the credit risks are mitigated. For innovative or unusual transactions, the underwriting process may need to be tailored to the unique risks of the transaction and involve a research and development phase. If a new asset type is involved, the process requires considerable research on its quality and performance under economic adversity.

At the conclusion of the underwriting process, the client receives an underwriting commitment subject to conditions deemed appropriate by the guarantor. If the commitment and its terms are accepted by the client, detailed negotiations of the transaction structure and documents follow until the ABS is priced, sold and closed.

Guarantors typically structure transactions to ensure that they will incur no losses. Their *modus operandi,* as well as their specific transaction requirements, are also geared to this end. They generally require that the expected loss on the underlying collateral is covered several-fold, through "first loss protection," which may take the form of over-collateralization, spread accounts, refundable or non-refundable cash deposits, or third-party recourse. Financial guarantees are considered to be "second loss protection," as they mitigate risks to a higher degree. (See Exhibit 4.)

To maintain their high portfolio asset quality, financial guarantors make certain that each ABS issue meets the rating agencies' investment grade standards in advance of issuing a surety bond. This contrasts with banks providing LOCs, CCAs or CIAs, which generally do not have this requirement and consequently are in a position to bear part or all of the first loss. This may change somewhat as banks providing credit enhancement come under a new "ratings-based" capital adequacy regime in the United States.

The due diligence process does not end here, however. Additional research and analysis are carried out to ascertain whether (1) the quality of the underlying assets is good, (2) the legal structure gives sound protection against subsequent challenge, (3) the transaction allows the guarantor to monitor the structure's performance with vigilance, (4) there is extensive regulatory oversight from the insurance regulators and the rating agencies, (5) the seller/servicer has a material stake in the event of a loss to provide it with a strong incentive to ensure the ongoing integrity of the structure, and (6) reinsurance is arranged, whenever appropriate, to diversify the guarantor's risks.

The time lapse between an initial inquiry and an underwriting commitment can range from several days for a simple secondary market guarantee of a portion of an outstanding ABS to a few months, which is closer to the norm. Routine transactions can be closed in several weeks — although the process can be accelerated if necessary. For unusual transactions, including those which deal with assets outside the United States, the process can take longer.

EXPOSURE MANAGEMENT AND RISK MONITORING

To protect their capital and the investors purchasing guaranteed securities, all financial guarantors are committed to ongoing monitoring and surveillance, both on a transaction basis and on an overall portfolio basis. After a transaction is closed, each company follows detailed procedures to monitor the performance of the collateral, the servicer and other related parties. The procedures can include on-site visits, audits, regular telephone contact, and written reports.

Most financial guarantee companies have designated individual departments responsible for monitoring and surveillance. The unit may also be responsible for ensuring that the legal documents are complete and safely stored, that all monitoring requirements are documented, analyzed and met and that audits are conducted and reviewed as required. Generally, each transaction is reviewed formally at least once a year, with more frequent reviews based on need. The monitoring unit draws on the company's systems and staff to identity problems, on a pro-active basis as appropriate, and correct them before they result in losses for the company.

In addition to transaction monitoring, financial guarantee companies evaluate and monitor portfolio risks. For example, one company maintains a database that permits it to analyze its structured finance portfolio exposure according to product types, issuers, geographic concentration, trustees, transaction structure, maturities, and a variety of other factors. With an exposure management and monitoring unit alert to economic and financial developments that could affect individual transactions and the overall portfolio, senior management has the ability to anticipate, evaluate, and correct problems to protect the company and the investors.

DIFFERING TYPES OF FINANCIAL GUARANTEES

While the basic type of financial guarantee covers all financial obligations of the issuer with respect to a guaranteed issue, there are many forms and variants. The simplest and most common form covers full payment of the principal and interest due to the investor from an ABS. In such transactions, investors need look no further than to the guarantor for payments, in the event of a default by the underlying obligor. While the prospectus for a guaranteed ABS may, subject to the applicable laws and regulations, disclose the general nature of the collateral and structure, it need not do so in great detail because the investor is taking the guarantor's risk.

An alternative form of guarantee is the "principal only" guarantee, which does not cover the interest payments of an ABS. Few transactions of this kind have been completed.

Some guarantors have guaranteed the credit risk of counterparties in derivative products such as interest rate or foreign currency swaps. In these transactions, the guarantor simply steps into the shoes of the counterparty should the latter fail to fulfill its swap or other similar obligations.

Other guarantors have provided "partial guarantees" for a security; that is, coverage of less than 100% of credit losses on the underlying asset pool, but enough to attain a triple-A rating. This type of guarantee is quite popular and competes directly with other forms of credit enhancement, including LOCs, CCAs or CIAs, and senior subordination.

Some financial guarantors have provided full guarantees for the subordinated tranches of securities, the credit risks of which are similar to those incurred in providing a partial guarantee on the entire pool. Market participants have occasionally shown a preference for such a structure, especially when market conditions make it difficult to sell unenhanced subordinated tranches.

Also, several guarantors have followed the example of secondary market guarantee programs instituted for municipal bonds and other securities by providing guarantees of secondary market tranches of asset backed securities as well as certain types of corporate obligations — for example, the first mortgage bonds of investor-owned utilities.

PREMIUMS FOR FINANCIAL GUARANTEES

Financial guarantors' premiums are determined in response to two factors: return on equity for the transaction and market factors, including value added and competition. The guarantors use either upfront premiums (the norm in municipal transactions) or ongoing premiums (the norm in ABS transactions) or a combination of the two. Upfront fees are sometimes waived with routine transactions in the ABS market, but with complex transactions they can be significant. Fees generally range from under 10 or 15 basis points per annum for commodity-type transactions in the United States' markets to more than 100 basis points for complex financing programs for low-rated seller/servicers with high quality assets. Most transaction premiums fall somewhere in between. The payment schedule for premiums usually mirrors the payment schedule for the underlying assets and/or securities, though this need not be the case.

The capital that the financial guarantee company must "earmark" for each transaction, the "capital charge", is a function of both rating agency guidelines and applicable state insurance regulations on leverage (see the earlier discussion of regulatory controls on guarantors). Capital which must be reserved is the higher of the amounts required according to the rating agencies on the one hand and the insurance regulators on the other.

The maximum premium that a financial guarantor can charge depends on the value it adds, including its speed of execution, expertise, trading levels, etc. This upper limit is determined by the cost, terms and availability of alternative forms of credit enhancement, and, indeed, any alternative cost of funds for the issuer.

The guarantor is thus able to set the premium based on the value added, the capital charge, and its target return on capital. In theory, the minimum acceptable premium for a given risk (which is determined by applying a return target to the capital charge) is the same for all financial guarantors. In practice, of course, actual premiums assigned vary among guarantors based on their differing perceptions of these factors and their willingness to compete on a given transaction.

THE ROLE OF REINSURERS

Reinsurance is used extensively by financial guarantee companies to diversify transaction and portfolio risks, increase underwriting capacity, and increase profitability ratios. Reinsurance improves profitability ratios because the risks retained are reduced more than the premiums earned.

A reinsurer takes a negotiated portion of the risk, typically on a pro-rata (as opposed to an "excess of loss") basis. This arrangement can be carried out on a transaction-by-transaction — or "facultative" — basis, or on a "treaty" basis, whereby eligible transactions are automatically reinsured by providers which are a party to the treaty. The financial guarantee company originating the transaction withholds a "ceding" commission to cover a portion of its originating and monitoring expenses.

MARKET SPREADS AND CREDIT ENHANCEMENT

Yields on ABS generally exceed those on unenhanced ("natural") triple-A corporate debt with similar maturity and credit characteristics. This is the case for two reasons. First, the paper issued by natural triple-A companies is scarce. Second, ABS cash flow characteristics, including scheduled and unscheduled principal payments and repayments, are generally less predictable than those of straight corporate debt. Naturally, investors demand a premium for cash flow uncertainty.

Spreads can also differ to a limited extent between similar financings supported by different types of credit enhancement. Where they exist, such differences reflect investor concerns on the perceived credit quality of a specific transaction, as determined by the collateral type, the seller/servicer, the structure, and perhaps the credit enhancement technique. When spreads differ among comparable issues backed by different financial guarantee companies, they may reflect perceptions about the company's capital adequacy, portfolio risk, parent support, and product expertise. However, it is not easy to isolate the spread impact of any one factor, including the credit enhancement technique or its provider.

CONCLUSION

Financial guarantee companies are generally not as well known or as large as international banks that provide credit enhancement. In order to further improve spreads on issues they insure, financial guarantee providers have continued to educate investors about their industry and its unparalleled track record of financial reliability. As a result, issuers and investors are becoming increasingly aware of the value added by financial guarantors, which includes triple-A credit quality, stringent underwriting procedures, vigilant regulatory supervision, and confidence inspired by the industry's successful history.

Financial guarantees represent an attractive credit enhancement technique widely accepted by issuers and investors. With the current growth in United States and international ABS markets, they constitute an economical means of mitigating risk and taking advantage of investment opportunities. Since the availability and applicability of credit enhancement alternatives vary as the capital markets continue to evolve, issuers, bankers, and investors will benefit from a better understanding of the role of financial guarantees in securitization.

Chapter 7

Accounting for Securitizations Under FASB 125

Marty Rosenblatt
Partner
Deloitte & Touche LLP

INTRODUCTION

The Financial Accounting Standards Board's Statement No. 125, *Accounting for Transfers and Servicing of Financial Assets and Extinguishments of Liabilities*, went into effect starting with 1997 transactions.[1] Previous FASB Statements (most notably FASB 77) did not anticipate or accommodate the continuous innovations in the securitization markets. The FASB's Emerging Issues Task Force has the job of trying to keep pace with the market.[2] FASB 125 together with some subsequent EITF consensuses and FASB and SEC staff announcements provides significantly greater structuring flexibility without "deal-breaking" accounting consequences.

WHEN FASB 125 APPLIES

FASB 125 applies to:

- public and private companies.
- public and private offerings.
- all transfers of financial assets, including transfers of debt and equity securities and direct financing leases.

---

[1] This chapter addresses only securitizations. It does not address other transactions covered by FASB 125 such as repos, dollar rolls, securities lending transactions, wash sales, loan syndications, loan participations, banker's acceptances, factoring arrangements, and debt extinguishments (including in-substance defeasances of debt).

[2] The FASB staff has codified the status of each prior EITF consensus affected by FASB 125. This can be found in Topic D-52 of the *EITF Abstracts*.

The author wishes to thank his partner, Jim Johnson, for his valuable contributions to this chapter. This chapter is intended as a guide only, and the application of its contents to specific situations will depend on the particular circumstances involved. At the time of this writing (June 1998), the FASB is considering significant amendments and interpretations of FASB 125. Accordingly, it is recommended that readers seek up-to-date information or professional advice regarding any particular problems that they encounter, and this guide should not be relied on as a substitute for this advice.

FASB 125 does not apply to:

- transfers of non-financial assets such as operating leases, servicing assets, stranded utility costs or sales of future revenues such as entertainers' royalty receipts.
- investor accounting rules (but see discussion of interest-only strips and other securities subject to prepayment risk).
- income tax sale versus borrowing characterizations or tax gain/loss calculations.[3]
- regulatory accounting or risk-based capital rules for depository institutions.[4]
- statutory accounting or risk-based capital rules for insurance companies.[5]
- accounting principles outside of the United States (but FASB 125 does apply to transactions by foreign subsidiaries in consolidated financial statements of U.S. multinationals).

QUESTIONS FOR SECURITIZATIONS UNDER FASB 125

When is a Securitization Accounted for as a Sale?

A securitization of a financial asset, a portion of a financial asset, or a pool of financial assets in which the transferor surrenders control over the assets transferred, is accounted for as a sale. The transferor is considered to have surrendered control in a securitization only if all three of the following conditions are met:

1. The transferred assets have been isolated from the transferor — put beyond the reach of the transferor and its creditors, even in the event of bankruptcy of the transferor. [9a][6]

---

[3] The Financial Asset Securitization Investment Trust (FASIT) tax legislation became effective September 1, 1997, but FASITS have not been a popular vehicle and regulations have not yet been issued.

[4] Federally-chartered banks are required to follow GAAP (i.e., FASB 125) when preparing *Call Reports*. However, pursuant to the risk-based capital rules, in asset sales where the bank provides recourse, the bank generally must hold capital for the full outstanding amount of the assets transferred. "Low-level recourse" limits the risk-based capital charge to the lower of (1) the bank's maximum contractual exposure under the recourse obligation (e.g., the book value of a spread account or subordinated security) or (2) the amount of capital that would have been required had the assets not been transferred. The OCC and the other bank regulatory agencies are currently considering the regulatory capital treatment for sales with recourse and are planning to issue a notice of proposed rulemaking on that subject.

[5] The National Association of Insurance Commissioners (NAIC) codification working group has generally endorsed, in Issues Paper No. 86, the securitization guidance in FASB 125 except (1) sales treatment is not permitted for transactions where recourse or call or put options exist and (2) servicing rights assets are non-admitted assets. "Recourse" for these purposes does not include the retention of a subordinated security in a securitization.

[6] Numbers within brackets refer to paragraph numbers of FASB 125.

This is a "facts and circumstances" determination which may include judgments about the kind of bankruptcy or other receivership into which a transferor or special-purpose entity might be placed, whether a transfer would likely be deemed a true sale at law and whether the transferor is affiliated with the transferee. In contrast to the "going-concern" convention in accounting, this possibility of bankruptcy must be dealt with, regardless of how remote it may seem in relation to the transferor's current credit standing. For example, a double-A rated issuer of auto paper must take steps to isolate the assets in the event of bankruptcy and cannot simply say that there is no way that bankruptcy could be a problem during the relatively short term of the securitization. [7]

2. The transferee is a "qualifying special-purpose entity" (see definition) and the holders of debt and equity interests in that entity have the right to pledge or exchange those *interests*. If the special-purpose entity is not a qualifying one, then sale accounting is only permitted if the special-purpose entity itself has the right to pledge or exchange the *transferred assets*. [9b]

The qualifying status of a special-purpose entity is extremely important because, generally, a qualifying SPE does not have to be consolidated, while a non-qualifying one may need to be consolidated.[8] Qualifying SPEs are basically designed to operate on "automatic pilot."[9] At inception, the SPE hires a servicer (generally the transferor) to collect payments on its assets. It also hires a trustee to administer and oversee its undertakings and may engage the services of an advisor to identify appropriate investments for temporary excess funds.

The substantive investor protection features of a highly rated securitization are designed to prevent the seller from altering significant terms without the consent of investors. Holders of an SPE's securities are sometimes limited in their ability to transfer their interests, due to a requirement to only transfer a security if an exemption from the requirements of the Securities Act of 1933 is available. Restrictions such as this, which accomplish tax or securities law objectives, will have to be analyzed to determine whether they constrain the transferee as a practical matter. The primary limitation imposed by Rule 144A — that a potential buyer must be a sophisticated investor — may not preclude sale accounting because it often would not constrain those holders from transferring their beneficial interests to any of a large number of qualified buyers and, thereby, realize the full economic benefit of the assets. The FASB has said that a transferor's right of first refusal on a bona fide offer from a third party, or a requirement to obtain the transferor's permission to sell or pledge that shall not be unreasonably withheld, generally does not constrain the transferee from exercising its right to pledge or exchange its interests. [25]

---

[7] See discussion below entitled "Why do the assets have to be isolated?"
[8] See discussion below entitled "Do I have to consolidate a QSPE?"
[9] See discussion of Qualifying SPEs.

3. The transferor does not effectively maintain control over the transferred assets by an agreement that entitles (or both entitles and obligates) the transferor to repurchase the transferred assets. [9c]

A cleanup call is permitted and is defined as: a purchase option held by the servicer, which may be the transferor, which is exercisable when the amount of outstanding assets falls to a level at which the cost of servicing those assets becomes burdensome.[10] [243] An agreement that both entitles and obligates the transferor to repurchase the transferred assets (e.g., an automatic rather than optional repurchase) maintains the transferor's effective control over those assets and therefore is generally accounted for as a secured borrowing. [27]

What About Puts and Calls?

No quantitative guidance on the size of a cleanup call is set forth in FASB 125. Generally 10% is viewed as the maximum for GAAP. Note that the definition states that the option is held by the servicer. The SEC Staff has said that call options on the debt or equity securities issued by the qualifying SPE have the same effect as call options on the transferred assets.[11]

If the transferred assets are readily obtainable elsewhere (such as Treasury bonds or widely traded corporate bonds), then a call option (regardless of size) will not disqualify sale treatment and certain forward repurchase agreements may not give the transferor effective control. [30] The theory here is that if the assets are readily obtainable elsewhere, the transferee can sell the transferred assets (thereby relinquishing the seller's "effective" control) and if the call option is exercised, the buyer can readily find suitable assets in sufficient quantity to satisfy the call. Although this is a more liberal provision than FASB 77, it does not offer much practical utility for the securitization of consumer loans. It is unlikely that an SPE would be permitted to sell the transferred assets and be able to buy substantially the same consumer loans acceptable to the transferor in the event the transferor exercises its call option.

In a very significant change from FASB 77, put options no longer disqualify sale treatment. For example, convertible ARMs could be securitized with a put back to the transferor, if the borrower converts (subject to meeting the other sale criteria). Short-term tranches could have a guaranteed final maturity in the form of a put to achieve "liquid asset" treatment for thrifts or "money market" treatment for certain classes of investors. In each of these cases, the transferor would have to record as a liability the fair value of the put obligation. If it is not practicable to estimate its fair value, no gain on sale can be recorded.

Also, asymmetrical principal distributions such as turbo-mechanisms, sequential-pay classes, controlled amortization or bullet payments in revolving structures can now be adopted in sale transactions. However, provisions which both entitle and obligate the transferor to re-acquire non-readily obtainable assets

---

[10] See further discussion of cleanup calls in the next section.
[11] Topic D-63 of the EITF Abstracts.

are considered forward commitments to repurchase and do not qualify for sale treatment. These differ from a put or call option because an option is volitional. If it is disadvantageous to the buyer to exercise its put rights, the buyer lets them lapse and can sell the assets at a better price in the open market. In a forward, the buyer is obligated to perform; it must return the assets. Consider, for example, 5/1 ARMS, in which the borrower's interest rate periodically adjusts after the initial 5-year fixed-rate period. If these loans were transferred for just the 5-year period, sale accounting would not be appropriate. However, a buyer put at the end of five years would be acceptable (subject to meeting the other sale criteria).

Do Revolving Structures Qualify?

Revolving structures do qualify. Moreover, some additional structuring flexibility exists. EITF 88-22 did not permit sale accounting if the liquidation method allowed the percentage of principal collections allocated to the investors to exceed their proportionate ownership interests in the receivables of the trust (at the beginning of the amortization period). FASB 125 does not carry over that restriction. Also, it is appropriate to recognize transaction costs over the initial and reinvestment periods in some systematic and rational manner, as opposed to all up-front (unless the future sales that are to occur during the revolving period are expected to result in recording a loss). At the time of this writing, the FASB is considering, but has not concluded on, whether a "removal of accounts" provision is akin to a call option that would disqualify sale treatment. In the meantime, follow EITF 90-18.

When is the Issuer a "*Qualifying*" Special-Purpose Entity?

A qualifying special-purpose entity (QSPE) must meet both conditions (a) and (b) below:

    a. It is a trust, corporation, or other legal vehicle whose activities are permanently limited to:

        1. Holding title to the transferred assets
        2. Issuing beneficial interests in the form of debt or equity securities. These include rights to receive all or portions of specified cash inflows, including senior and subordinated rights to interest or principal inflows to be "passed through" (e.g., multiclass participation certificates) or "paid through" (e.g., notes or bonds) and residual interests.
        3. Collecting cash proceeds from assets held, reinvesting in eligible investments pending distribution, and perhaps servicing the assets held.
        4. Distributing proceeds to the holders of its beneficial interests.

    b. It has standing at law distinct from the transferor. If the transferor holds all of the beneficial interests, the trust has no standing at law, is not distinct, and thus is not a QSPE and the transaction is neither a sale nor a financing. The true test here is whether the transferor gives up the ability to unilaterally dissolve the trust and reclaim the individual assets.[26] Special-purpose entities that issue debt or equity interests to parties unaffiliated with the transferor usually meet the condition of having standing at law distinct from the transferor because the transferor may not dissolve the entity without any involvement by the third-party holders of the beneficial interests.

As noted above, a QSPE may service the assets sold. This does not mean that the entity must itself perform the physical activity of servicing the financial assets. The special-purpose entity may engage another party, including the transferor, to perform the servicing of its assets. In addition to engaging a servicer, dismissing a servicer also would be considered within a QSPE's limited powers of servicing the assets held, if such powers were specified in the entity's charter. While these activities may require management involvement, they involve support and not financial activities, and thus, are permitted.

A QSPE is also limited to holding only financial assets. Therefore, any special-purpose entity receiving nonfinancial assets, such as unguaranteed residual values in direct financing leases or financial liabilities that are not beneficial interests issued by the entity, would not be considered a QSPE.

The accounting literature does not specify whether a QSPE is permitted to hold derivatives. However, most accountants take the view that a QSPE is permitted to hold derivatives, even those where the transferor is the counterparty, provided the derivative or an executory contract for the derivative is entered into concurrently with the transfer of the financial assets, the derivative does not affect the bankruptcy remote status of the special-purpose entity, and the derivative does not require future decision making by the special-purpose entity (i.e., as with certain options). These derivatives are entered into generally for the protection of the holders of the beneficial interests or to change the characteristics of the transferred assets and fall under the activity of servicing the assets held.

An example of a derivative entered into by a special-purpose entity is an interest rate swap. If the special-purpose entity purchases fixed-rate assets and issues variable-rate beneficial interests, the entity may enter into a "pay fixed/receive variable" interest rate swap with the transferor or a third party at the inception of the transfer to provide protection to investors against changes in interest rates. Provided the swap was entered into concurrent with the purchase of financial assets, the swap would not preclude the entity from being a qualifying special-purpose entity.

As another example, if the special-purpose entity does not enter into the derivative concurrent with the transfer but rather into an executory contract concurrent with the transfer that provides that a derivative automatically will be executed upon the occurrence of a future event, the subsequent execution of the derivative does not preclude the special-purpose entity from qualifying. In this situation, the execution of the swap was not discretionary and was provided for concurrent with the transfer. As noted above, activities of a qualifying special-purpose entity include issuing beneficial interests, and there is no requirement to issue all these interests at the same time. Future issuances or rollover of beneficial interests would not preclude a special-purpose entity from being considered qualifying if the future issuances are permitted under the governing trust documents, the future issuances occur automatically and there is sufficient liquidity or back-up provider in the event the reissuance is not possible.

Do I Have to Consolidate a QSPE?

FASB 125 does not provide any guidance on consolidation of SPEs. The FASB had hoped to issue a new *Statement on Consolidations* simultaneously with FASB 125, but was unable to do so. The off-balance sheet goal of a securitization would be defeated if the securitizer is required to consolidate the accounts of the SPE to which the assets are ultimately transferred, particularly if the SPE has issued debt securities. For example, consider the transaction in which you structure a securitization that clearly meets all three criteria for a sale, using a qualifying wholly-owned SPE that issues debt and equity interests, and then proceed to consolidate the SPE. The transferred assets re-emerge on the balance sheet. Contrast this with simply accounting for the retained interests in the securitization (in form, equity interests in the SPE) as a residual financial asset.

Fortunately, the EITF addressed this issue before the January 1, 1997 FASB 125 deadline. In Issue 96-20, they reached the following consensus:

If the SPE:

1. meets all of the conditions of paragraph 26 of FASB 125 to be a qualifying SPE
2. holds only financial assets such as receivables from credit cards, mortgage loans or securities that represent a contractual right to cash (or another financial instrument) from, or an ownership interest in, an entity that is unrelated to the transferor
3. does not undertake a transaction (or a series of transactions) that has the effect of (a) converting nonfinancial assets, for example, real estate or servicing assets, into a financial asset or (b) recognizing a previously unrecognized financial asset, for example, an operating lease;

then the transferor has surrendered control over the financial assets and consolidation is not appropriate regardless of whether the SPE is wholly-owned or whether it has any equity. FASB and EITF developments should be monitored for additional guidance.

Otherwise, the sponsor, creator, or transferor should consolidate majority-owned entities pursuant to ARB 51 and FASB 94 and should apply the consolidation criteria of EITF Abstracts, Topic D-14 (for SPEs which are not owned by, but may nevertheless be controlled by, the sponsor) and EITF 90-15 (for certain leasing transactions) to determine whether the SPE should be consolidated.

Topic D-14 of the EITF Abstracts addressed certain characteristics of transactions that raise questions about whether special-purpose entities should be consolidated. That guidance concluded that, for nonconsolidation by the sponsor or transferor to be appropriate, the majority owner of the special-purpose entity must be an independent third party that has made a substantial capital investment (in practice, a substantial investment has been held to be at least 3% of the assets transferred to the special-purpose entity), the majority owner has control over the special-purpose entity, and the owner has substantial risks and rewards in the ownership of the assets of the special-purpose entity. Conversely, nonconsolidation is not appropriate by the sponsor or transferor when the majority owner of the special-purpose entity makes only a nominal capital investment (less than 3% of the assets), the activities of the special-purpose entity are virtually all on the sponsor's or transferor's behalf, and the substantive risks and rewards of the assets or the debt of the special-purpose entity rest directly or indirectly with the sponsor or transferor. It was also concluded that nonconsolidation is not appropriate where the accounting for a transaction would change only because a special-purpose entity was placed between the two parties to the transaction.

Is it Possible to Structure Debt for Tax as a Sale for GAAP?

I find that the securitization term "debt-for-tax" means different things to different people. In its most advanced state, the securitizer seeks to meet all of the following objectives, not simply the first one:

1. The securities being issued are characterized as debt of the issuer rather than equity in order to avoid "double taxation."
2. The transaction is treated as a financing by the transferor for tax purposes. This is accomplished by including the assets and debt of the issuer in a consolidated tax return of the transferor which results in deferring an upfront tax on any economic gain realized in the securitization.
3. Notes or bonds rather than pass-through certificates are issued so as to invite easier participation and eligibility for certain investor classes such as ERISA plans.
4. The transaction is treated as an "off-balance sheet" sale for accounting purposes with recognition of any attendant gain and without consolidation of the issuer into the financial statements of the transferor.

To meet the accounting objective, I suggest you follow the following guidelines:

1. The issuer needs to be a "qualifying special-purpose entity" (QSPE) as defined in FASB 125, paragraph 26, amplified by paragraph 125 of FASB 125 and required by EITF 96-20 (to avoid consolidation). Some say that this means it has to be "brain-dead," on "automatic pilot," and "it is not allowed to think." Note that in a two-tier structure, the entity that issues the debt (e.g., the trust) needs to be the QSPE. The "intermediate

SPEs" (e.g., the depositor), are typically not considered QSPEs. As long as the "issuing SPE" is a QSPE, the nature of the intermediate entities will not typically affect the accounting treatment for consolidation purposes.

2. The legal form of the QSPE does not matter. It can be an owner trust, partnership, corporation, etc.
3. There is no minimum size requirement for the equity of the QSPE for accounting purposes, but check with your tax advisors.
4. The equity of the QSPE can be wholly owned by the transferor.
5. The assets transferred to the QSPE must all be financial assets and generally no transfer can have occurred prior to 1997, but see EITF 97-6 if a pre-existing QSPE is used.
6. The transfer of assets to the QSPE must meet the sale accounting requirements of FASB 125. The critical factor here is that the lawyers will be asked to give a "would" opinion on the question of isolation of assets in the event of bankruptcy of the transferor or its affiliates.
7. Put options may be fine if the bankruptcy lawyers say they're fine (see 6).
8. Call options are problematic. Generally, the issuer and the tax lawyers want substantive call provisions and the accountants and underwriters do not. In a letter dated July 23, 1997, the Chief Accountant of the SEC announced that call options on the bonds should be viewed the same way as call options on the transferred assets; that is, the use of such call options would be considered inconsistent with the sale accounting requirements of FASB 125. In practice, a "safe-harbor" has emerged at the 10% level to qualify as a cleanup call provided the transferor or an affiliate is the servicer.

The nonconsolidation of qualifying SPEs has somewhat reduced the tension that often existed between accountants and tax lawyers when trying to structure a "debt-for-tax/sale-for-GAAP" deal. It has also allowed for the issuance of collateralized debt securities by qualifying SPEs rather than some form of hybrid debt/participation certificate. The tax lawyers take into consideration the following factors in determining whether a transaction should be treated as a financing and some of the factors are given greater weight than others:

1. A revolving period of at least one year.
2. A partial reinvestment of principal collections in newly originated collateral for at least three years.
3. Payment mismatch (e.g., monthly pay collateral and quarterly pay debt).
4. Use of excess spread to pay principal on debt.
5. Existence and the size of the present value of the equity in the issuing entity.
6. Nomenclature used in the transaction (i.e., calling the securities bonds or notes).

7. Interest rate cap (i.e., a debt-like cap at an objective rate or an equity-like cap at the weighted average rate of receivables).
8. Right of the issuer to call the debt at a point significantly earlier than a typical cleanup call. (See warning above.)
9. Use of a different floating-rate index for interest on the debt other than the index on the underlying loans.

Why Do the Assets Have to be Isolated?

While the benefits of asset isolation are no doubt laudatory, why has the FASB incorporated this notion as a condition for sale accounting? The Board explains its decision as follows:

> Credit rating agencies and investors pay close attention to the possibility of bankruptcy of the transferor, its affiliates or the special-purpose entity, even though the possibility may seem unlikely, because those are major risks to them. If receivers can reclaim securitized assets, investors will suffer a delay in payments due them, and may be forced to attempt a pro rata settlement. Credit rating agencies and investors commonly demand transaction structures to minimize those possibilities. They also seek assurances from attorneys about whether entities can be forced into receivership, what the powers of the receiver might be, and whether the transaction structure would withstand receivers' attempts to reach the securitized assets in ways that would harm investors. Unsatisfactory structures or assurances could result in credit ratings that are lower than those of the transferor's liabilities, and, in lower prices for transferred assets. [118]

Many securitizations use two transfers to isolate transferred assets beyond the reach of the transferor and its creditors:

> *Step 1:* The corporation transfers assets to a special-purpose corporation (SPC) that, although wholly-owned, is designed so that the chance of the transferor, or its creditors, reclaiming the assets is remote. The first transfer is designed to be judged a true sale at law, in part because it does not provide credit or yield protection.

> *Step 2:* The SPC transfers the assets to a trust, with a sufficient increase in the credit and yield protection on the second transfer, to merit the high credit rating sought by investors. The second transfer may or may not be judged a true sale at law and, in theory, could be reached by a bankruptcy trustee for the SPC. However, its charter forbids it from undertaking any other business or incurring any liabilities, so that there can be no creditors (other than any arising from the securitization itself) to petition to

place it in bankruptcy. Accordingly, the SPC is designed to lessen the possibility that it would enter bankruptcy, either by itself or as part of a bankruptcy of its parent. [57]

A one-tier structure with significant continuing involvement by the transferor might not satisfy the isolation test. A trustee in bankruptcy of the transferor might find the transfer to not be a true sale, in such circumstances, and has substantial powers to alter amounts that investors might receive.

Generally, the standard for isolation of assets would be met if it is concluded that:

1. The transfer from the originator to the subsidiary SPE constitutes a true sale.
2. The SPE on one hand, and its affiliates that are not SPEs or depository institutions on the other hand, would not be substantively consolidated in the case of the bankruptcy of any such applicable affiliate.
3. The final transfer from the consolidated group is either a true sale or the transfer of a first priority, perfected security interest in the transferred assets.[12]

Investment bankers are "exporting" securitization know-how overseas. Any company or subsidiary — regardless of location — that prepares financial statements in accordance with US GAAP, must adequately isolate securitized assets (and meet the other conditions of FASB 125) to achieve sale accounting. Whether assets have been isolated will depend on an evaluation of laws in the jurisdiction governing the transaction. The advice of counsel familiar with local laws is especially important.

Isolation of Assets Transferred by Financial Institutions

When FASB issued FASB 125, it understood that the FDIC had broad powers to terminate certain transactions (and reclaim transferred assets) in the event an institution failed. However, FASB understood that, under FDIC policy, investors would receive compensation equivalent to all principal and interest earned to the date the payment was made. Such an arrangement only would make an investor whole for contractual cash flows to the date of the payment. The arrangement would still leave the investor at risk for increases in the fair value of the asset which is based on future cash flows. Unfortunately, the FASB's understanding may not have been correct and the FDIC may have broader powers. For U.S. banks insured by the FDIC, the FASB now notes that an FDIC receiver has power to reclaim transferred assets by paying interest only to the date of receivership (and *not* to the date of "payment").

At the January EITF meeting, the FASB staff made an announcement dealing with this issue (cited as Topic D-67 in the *EITF Abstracts*). Topic D-67 includes the following guidance:

---

[12] See the later discussion on "Do I always need a lawyer's letter?"

- The FASB staff believes it is reasonable for constituents in interpreting the provisions of Statement 125 to have concluded that the powers of the FDIC to reclaim transferred assets by paying principal plus interest should not preclude sale accounting for those transfers under paragraph 9(a) of the Statement.
- Until the FASB staff completes its investigation and issues additional guidance, it believes that it is not reasonable to expect constituents to change their interpretation of Statement 125 to conclude that the power of the FDIC to reclaim transferred assets should preclude sale accounting under paragraph 9(a) of the Statement.

One possible outcome of the FASB's continuing investigation may be to (1) revise its previously stated understanding of the powers of the FDIC and, therefore, (2) change its assessment that one-tier structures used by financial institutions subject to FDIC receivership may meet the isolation requirements of FAS 125.

Do I Always Need a Lawyer's Letter?

In late 1997, the American Institute of Certified Public Accountants issued an interpretation of generally accepted auditing standards, *The Use of Legal Interpretations as Evidential Matter to Support Management's Assertion that a Transfer of Financial Assets Has Met the Isolation Criteria in Paragraph 9 (a) of Statement of Financial Accounting Standards No. 125.*

The Interpretation contains an extract of a legal opinion (for an entity that is subject to the U.S. Bankruptcy Code) that provides persuasive evidence (in the absence of contradictory evidence) to support management's assertion that the transferred assets have been isolated. In short, it is a true sale *would* opinion versus a *should* or *more likely than not* opinion. This represents the highest level of assurance counsel is able to provide on the question of isolation. The example is as follows:

We believe [or it is our opinion] that in a properly presented and argued case, as a legal matter, in the event the Seller were to become a Debtor, the transfer of the Financial Assets from the Seller to the Purchaser [e.g., a QSPE] *would* be considered to be a sale [or a true sale] of the Financial Assets from the Seller to the Purchaser and not a loan and, accordingly, the Financial Assets and the proceeds thereof transferred to the Purchaser by the Seller in accordance with the Purchase Agreement would not be deemed to be property of the Seller's estate for purposes of [the relevant sections] of the U.S. Bankruptcy Code.

...Based upon the assumptions of fact and the discussion set forth above, and on a reasoned analysis of analogous case law, we are of the opinion that in a properly presented and argued case, as a legal matter, in a proceeding under the U.S. Bankruptcy Code, in which the Seller is a Debtor, a court *would not* grant an order consolidating the assets and liabilities of the Purchaser [e.g., the QSPE] with those of the Seller in a case involving the insolvency of the Seller under the doctrine of substantive consolidation. [If an affiliate of the Seller has entered into transactions with the Purchaser, the opinion should address that.]

The above example deals with a one-step transfer of financial assets. In a two-step transfer, lawyer's opinions should also address the second transfer (from the wholly-owned bankruptcy remote subsidiary to the securitization vehicle that issues beneficial interests to investors. In most securitizations that feature credit enhancement (for example, the wholly owned bankruptcy remote subsidiary retains a subordinated interest in the securitization vehicle), the lawyer's letter usually cannot conclude that the second transfer is a true sale. Instead, the attorney usually concludes that this transfer would either be a true sale or a secured financing.

Other issues covered in the Auditing Interpretation are listed in Exhibit 1. The Interpretation does not apply to securitizations by FDIC-insured institutions.

Can a QSPE Ever Sell its Assets?

The FASB staff provided guidance in an announcement at the January 1998 EITF meeting (documented in the *EITF Abstracts* as Topic D-66). Topic D-66 addresses the effect of a special-purpose entity's powers to sell, exchange, repledge, or distribute transferred financial assets under FASB 125 (collectively these are referred to below as the "powers" of a QSPE). Although Topic D-66 restricts the powers of a QSPE, it permits more activities than (1) many observers of the standard setting process predicted it would or (2) the FASB staff would have tolerated in a preliminary announcement it made in November 1997.

Topic D-66 allows an SPE to exercise a power to sell, exchange, repledge or distribute transferred financial assets in response to a clean-up call or if all of four stipulated conditions exist. As will be seen, the conditions prevent a securitizer from transferring "off balance sheet" all or a portion of its managed investment or trading portfolio. The conditions also block an end run around FAS 125's prohibition on achieving sale accounting when the seller has effective control over the transferred assets.

The four conditions follow and some of the Topic D-66 examples are included in Exhibit 2.

1. The powers and the conditions or events that permit them to be exercised are specified in and limited permanently by the legal documents that (a) establish the SPE or (b) initially create the beneficial interests in the transferred assets that are subject to the powers.

Exhibit 1: Other Issues Covered in the Auditing Interpretation

Question	Key Points
What should the auditor consider in determining whether to use the work of a legal specialist to obtain persuasive evidence to support management's assertion that a transfer of assets meets the isolation criterion of FASB 125?	• Use of a legal specialist may not be necessary when there is a routine transfer of financial assets without continuing involvement by the seller (e.g., full or limited recourse, servicing, other retained interests in the transferred assets or an equity interest in the transferee). • Use of a legal specialist usually is necessary if, in the auditor's judgment, the transfer involves complex legal structures, continuing seller involvement or other legal issues that make it difficult to determine whether the isolation criterion is met. • The auditor should evaluate the need for updates to a legal opinion if transfers occur over an extended period of time or if management asserts that a new transaction is the same as a prior structure. • A legal specialist may be a client's internal or external attorney who is knowledgeable about relevant sections of the law.
If the auditor determines that the use of a legal specialist is required, what should he or she consider in assessing the adequacy of the legal opinion?	• The auditor should consider whether the legal specialist has experience with relevant matters such as knowledge of the U.S. Bankruptcy Code and other applicable foreign or domestic laws and knowledge of the transaction. • A specialist's conclusion about hypothetical transactions generally would not provide persuasive evidence because it may not be relevant to the actual transaction nor contemplate all of the facts and circumstances or the provisions in the agreements of the actual transaction.
Are legal opinions that restrict the use of the opinion to the client or to third parties other than the auditor acceptable audit evidence?	No. The auditor should request that the client obtain the legal specialist's written permission for the auditor to use the opinion.
If the auditor determines that it is appropriate to use the work of a legal specialist, and either the resulting legal response does not provide persuasive evidence...or the legal specialist does not grant permission for the auditor to use a legal opinion that is restricted..., what other steps might an auditor consider?	• Because isolation is assessed primarily from a legal perspective, the auditor usually will not be able to obtain persuasive evidence in a form other than a legal opinion. • In the absence of persuasive evidence, derecognition of the transferred assets is not in conformity with generally accepted accounting principles and the auditor should consider the need to modify his or her opinion.

Exhibit 2: Limited Powers of a QSPE Specified in the Original Governing Documents

Powers that enable the SPE to sell its assets or put them back to the transferor	
Examples Consistent with QSPE Status	Examples Inconsistent with QSPE Status
The SPE has the power to either (a) "put" the transferred assets back to the transferor or (b) sell those assets in response to (1) a default by the obligor, (2) a major third-party rating agency downgrade of the transferred assets or the underlying obligor to a rating below a specified minimum rating, or (3) a decline in the fair value of the transferred assets to a value significantly less than their fair value at the time they were transferred to the SPE.	The transferor has the power, either directly or indirectly, to trigger a condition that enables an SPE to sell the transferred assets (unless the triggering of the condition would have a significant adverse consequence to the transferor).
The SPE has the power to sell transferred assets (or to "put" transferred assets to the servicer, to a third party, or back to the transferor) in response to a failure by the transferor to properly service transferred assets that could result in the loss of a substantial third-party credit guaranty.	The SPE is required to return transferred assets back to the transferor upon the occurrence of an event that at the time of the initial transfer is *probable* to occur (unless that transfer back would result in significant adverse consequences to the transferor).
	The SPE has the power to sell transferred assets in response to a transferor's decision to exit a market or a particular activity.
	The SPE has the power to sell transferred assets in response to the transferor violating a nonsubstantive contractual provision.
The beneficial interest holders in an SPE *other than the transferor* may "put" their beneficial interests in the transferred assets back to the SPE in exchange for (1) a full or partial distribution of those assets, (2) cash (which may require that the SPE sell those assets to the transferor or a third party or issue beneficial interests to comply with the put), or (3) new beneficial interests in those assets.	The SPE is obligated to sell transferred assets under an option contract written by the SPE that entitles parties other than the third-party beneficial interest holders to "call" those assets and, under that arrangement, permits the SPE to trigger a sale and effectively recognize an appreciation in the fair value of the transferred assets.
"Auction Calls"	
Example Consistent with QSPE Status	Example Inconsistent with QSPE Status
The SPE's original legal documents schedule a sale or an auction of the transferred assets at the end of the life of either the SPE or the beneficial interests in the transferred assets; the transferor is precluded from bidding an amount above fair value for the transferred assets and the sale or auction includes obtaining bona fide offers from participants other than the transferor. However, a pattern of the transferor obtaining transferred assets through scheduled sales or auctions would suggest that they are bidding amounts greater than fair value and, therefore, maintaining effective control over the transferred assets.	The SPE's original legal documents schedule a sale or an auction of the transferred assets at the end of the life of either the SPE or the beneficial interests in the transferred assets and the transferor (1) is not precluded from bidding an amount higher than fair value and (2) retains the residual interest in an SPE entitling it to receive all of the resulting gain from the sale of transferred assets.

2. The powers do not result in the transferor or its affiliates maintaining effective control over the transferred assets or over the sale of those assets.

3. The primary objectives of the powers is not to realize a gain in the fair value of the transferred assets above their fair value at the time they were transferred to the SPE. Also, those powers do not permit the transferor, its affiliates, or the SPE the discretion to sell transferred assets to maximize the return to all or some of the beneficial interest holders. This condition does not preclude beneficial interest holders other than the transferor and its affiliates from having the ability to put their beneficial interests back to the SPE and, thereby, trigger the sale or distribution of assets.

4. The powers do not permit active or frequent selling and buying of assets.

Under the FASB staff's interpretation, an SPE is not *qualifying* if it can sell instruments in which cash reserves are reinvested for purposes of realizing a gain or otherwise maximizing the return to some portion of the beneficial interest holders. Also not qualifying is an SPE that is empowered to actively manage its temporarily invested cash reserves by selling and reinvesting. Note that the staff's interpretation does not limit the type of instruments in which to reinvest temporary cash.

As an example, suppose an SPE has cash balances that will not be distributed to beneficial interest holders for 200 days. The documents that establish the SPE give it the discretion, in these circumstances, to choose between investing in commercial paper obligations that mature in 90 or 180 days. This discretion does not preclude the SPE from being qualifying. If, in these circumstances, the SPE also had the discretion to invest in 360 day commercial paper with the intent to sell it in 200 days, the SPE is not qualifying.

The FASB plans to consider further the effect of an SPE's powers to sell, exchange, repledge, or distribute transferred financial assets on the accounting for transfers and to issue a proposed interpretation or amendment of FASB 125. Whether any resulting amendment or interpretation of FASB 125 would retain the views expressed in the FASB staff announcement D-66 is uncertain at this time.

QUESTIONS RELATING TO DETERMINING GAIN OR LOSS ON SALES

What if the Transfer Does Not Qualify as a Sale?

If the transfer does not qualify as a sale, assets or securities will remain on the balance sheet and the proceeds raised will be accounted for as a secured borrowing, with no gain or loss recognized. [12] Certain securitization transactions that are designed to recognize a loss, for tax purposes, with borrowing treatment for accounting purposes using consolidated subsidiaries, have been affected by the outcome of the consolidation decision referred to above. Those transactions will have to rely on a significant call option or a restriction on the ability of the holders of debt of the SPE from having the right to pledge or exchange their interests, in order to be accounted for as financings.

And if it Does Qualify as a Sale?

"Gain on sale" accounting (as it is sometimes described in practice) or loss on sale accounting is not elective. It is not appropriate for the transferor to defer any portion of a resulting gain or loss. (See the discussion below if it is not practicable to estimate the fair value of assets obtained or liabilities incurred.)

If the transfer qualifies as a sale, then:

1. Allocate the previous book carrying amount (net of loss reserves, if any) between the assets sold and the retained interests, if any, based on their relative fair values on the date of transfer. Allocation effectively defers a portion of the profit or loss — the amount attributable to the portion(s) of the financial asset retained.
2. Adjust the net cash proceeds received in the exchange by recording, in the balance sheet, the fair value of any guarantees, recourse obligations or derivatives such as put options written, forward commitments, interest rate or foreign currency swaps. No guidance is given in FASB 125 regarding the continuing accounting for these derivative-type financial instruments.
3. Recognize gain or loss only on the assets sold.
4. Continue to carry, on the balance sheet, any retained interest in the transferred assets, including a servicing asset, beneficial debt or equity instruments in the SPE or retained undivided interests. [10 and 11]

There is no provision that the amount of gain recognized on a partial sale cannot exceed the gain that would be recognized if the entire loan was sold. The FASB indicated that imposing such a limitation would have, among other things, resulted in ignoring the added value (i.e. arbitrage) that many believe is created when assets are divided into their several parts. [214]

Exhibit 3 provides an example of a gain on sale worksheet or template.

What if I Can't Reasonably Estimate Losses?

Under FASB 77, to be eligible for sale accounting, you needed to be able to reasonably estimate your losses under the recourse provisions. This is not a requirement under FASB 125. In the event it is not practicable to estimate the fair value of a retained asset, it should be valued at zero. In the event that it is not practicable to estimate the fair value of any liability, you will not be able to recognize any gain on sale. You may be required to record a loss if a liability under FASB 5 and FASB Interpretation 14 ("Reasonable Estimation of the Amount of a Loss") would be recognized. [45]

Exhibit 3: An Example of a Gain on Sale Worksheet or Template

Assumptions (all amounts are hypothetical and the relationships between amounts do not purport to be representative of actual transactions):
- *Aggregate Principal Amount of Pool* $100,000,000
- *Net carrying amount* (Principal amount + accrued interest $99,000,000
  + purchase premiums + deferred origination costs −
  deferred origination fees − purchase discount - loss
  reserves)
- *Deal Structure:*

	Principal Amount	Price	Fair Value*
Class A	$96.000,000	100	$96,000,000
Class B	4,000,000	95	3,800,000
Class IO			1,500,000
Class R			1,000,000
Total	$100,000,000		$102,300,000

*Including accrued interest
- Class IO and R are retained by the Seller
- Servicing Value: $700,000
- Up-front Transaction costs (underwriting, legal, accounting, rating agency, printing, etc.) $1,000,000

Basis Allocation of Carrying Value:

Component	Fair Value	% of Total Fair Value	($99MM x%) Allocated Carrying Amount	Sold
Servicing	$700,000	0.68 %	$673,200	
Class A	96,000,000	93.20	92,268,000	$92,268,000
Class B	3,800,000	3.69	3,653,100	3,653,100
Class IO	1,500,000	1.46	1,445,400	
Class R	1,000,000	0.97	960,300	
Total	$103,000,000	100.00 %	$99,000,000	$95,921,100
Net proceeds (with accrued interest, after $1 million transaction costs)				98,800,000
Pre-Tax Gain				$2,878,900

Journal Entries:	Debit	Credit
(1) Cash	$98,800,000	
Servicing Asset	673,200	
Class IO	1,445,400	
Class R	960,300	
Net carrying value of Loans		$99,000,000
Pre-tax gain on sale		2,878,900
(2) Class IO	$54,600	
Class R	39,700	
Equity (Earnings, if trading)		$94,300

In the second journal entry, the allocated carrying amount of Class IO and Class R are adjusted upward to their fair values because they are required to be classified as either an available for sale or trading security. [39]

When a securitizer concludes that it is not practicable to estimate fair values, FASB 125 requires footnote disclosure describing the related items and the reasons why it is not practicable to estimate their fair value. Practicable means that an estimate of fair value can not be made without incurring excessive costs. It is a dynamic concept: what is practicable for one entity might not be for another; what is not practicable in one year might be in another. [211]

How is Gain or Loss Determined in a Revolving Structure?

Gain or loss recognition for revolving-period receivables sold to a securitization trust is limited to receivables that exist and have been sold. Recognition of servicing assets is also limited to the servicing for the receivables that exist and have been sold. [52] It is expected that an allocation of the carrying amount of the receivables transferred to the SPE, and the retained interests (based on relative fair value) be performed. Exhibit 4 provides a credit card example.

A revolving securitization involves a large initial transfer of balances generally accounted for as a sale and then ongoing, smaller subsequent months' transfers (we like to call them "transferettes") are each treated as separate sales of new balances with the attendant gain or loss calculation, unless immaterial to the financial statements taken as a whole. The record keeping burden necessary to comply with these techniques is quite sizable, particularly for master trusts. Paragraph 46 of FASB 125 shows an example where the seller finds it impracticable to estimate the fair value of the servicing contract, although it is confident that servicing revenues will be more than adequate compensation for performing the servicing.

The implicit forward contract to sell new receivables during a revolving period, which may become valuable or onerous as interest rates and other market conditions change, is to be recognized at its fair value at the time of sale. Its value at inception will be zero if entered into at the market rate. For example, if the coupon to investors in a trust is a market rate of 6%, and later market rates of return for those investments increased to 7%, the forward contract's value to the transferor (and burden to the investors) would approximate the present value of the 1% of the amount of the investment for each year remaining in the revolving structure, after the balances already transferred have been collected. Of course, changes in the fair value of the forward contract are likely to be greater in fixed-rate rather than floating-rate deals. [50 and 51]

The discussion cited above has concerned many securitizers. Does FASB 125 require securitizers (especially those featuring revolvers in fixed-rate deals) to mark the forward to fair value in each accounting period following the securitization? FASB 125 contains no such requirement (it only deals with the subsequent accounting for servicing assets and certain assets subject to prepayment risk). Further, other sources of current GAAP do not deal with commitments of this nature.

Exhibit 4: Credit Card Example

Assumptions (all amounts are hypothetical and the relationships between amounts do not purport to be representative of actual transactions):

• Aggregate Principal Amount of Pool	$650,000,000
• Carrying amount, net of specifically allocated loss reserve	637,000,000
• Servicing Value	5,000,000
• Value of fixed-price forward contract for future sales	0
• Up-front transaction costs	4,000,000
• Losses are reimbursed from excess interest spread account	
• Deal Structure:	

	Principal Amount	Price	Fair Value
Class A	$500,000,000	100	$500,000,000
Class B	25,000,000	100	25,000,000
Seller's Certificate	125,000,000		125,000,000
IO Strip*			10,000,000
Servicing			5,000,000
Total	$650,000,000		$665,000,000

Basis Allocation of Carrying Value

Component	Fair Value	Percent of Total Fair Value	($637MM x%) Allocated Carrying Amount	Sold	Retained
Class A	$500,000,000	75.19	$478.960,300	$478,960,300	
Class B	25,000,000	3.76	23,951,200	23,951,200	
Seller Certificate	125,000,000	18.80	119,756,000	**	$119,756,000
IO Strip*	10,000,000	1.50	9,555,000		9.555.000
Servicing	5,000,000	.75	4,777,500		4,777,500
Total	$665,000,000	100.00	$637,000,000	$502,911,500	$134,088,500

Proceeds net of allocated transaction costs (assume 25%)	$524,000,000
Pre-tax Gain	$21,088,500

Journal Entries:	Debit	Credit
(1) Cash	$521,000,000	
IO Strip	9,555,000	
Servicing Asset	4,777,500	
Seller's Certificate	119,756,000**	
Deferred transaction costs	3,000,000	
Net carrying amount of loans		$637,000,000
Pre-tax gain		21,088,500
(2) IO Strip	$445,000	
Equity		$445,000

* In determining the fair value of the IO Strip, the seller would consider the yield on the receivables, charge-off rates, average life of the transferred balances and the subordination of the IO flows in a spread account.

** Note that in the above example, the allocated carrying amount of the Seller's Certificate is less than its principal balance. FASB 125 does not provide any guidance on how such difference should be amortized. Presumably, it should be amortized as additional yield over the average life of the retained balances.

Each month during the revolving period, the investor's share of principal collections would be used to purchase new receivable balances ("transferettes") and an analysis similar to the above would be made with a new gain recorded. The recordkeeping burden to comply with these techniques is sizable, particularly for master trusts.

Is Fair Value in the Eyes of the "B-Holder"?

FASB 125 does not introduce any new accounting definition of fair value. The fair value of an asset or liability is defined as the amount at which it could be bought or sold (or settled), in a current transaction between willing parties, other than in a forced or liquidation sale. Quoted market prices in active markets are the best evidence of fair value and should be used as the basis for the measurement, whenever available. [42] If quoted market prices are not available, the estimate of fair value should be based on the best information available. The estimate of fair value should consider prices for similar instruments and the results of valuation techniques, such as: the present value of the estimated future cash flows using a discount rate commensurate with the risks involved, option-pricing models, OAS, and matrix pricing. [43]

It would be unusual for a securitizer to find quoted market prices for most financial components arising in a securitization — complicating the measurement process and requiring estimation techniques. FASB 125 discusses these situations as follows:

- The underlying assumptions about interest rates, default rates, prepayment rates and volatility should reflect what market participants would use.
- Estimates of expected future cash flows should be based on reasonable and supportable assumptions and projections.
- All available evidence should be considered, and the weight given to the evidence should be commensurate with the extent to which the evidence can be verified objectively.
- If a range is estimated for either the amount or timing of possible cash flows, the likelihood of all possible outcomes should be considered in determining the best estimate of future cash flows. [44]

In the fourth quarter of 1997, a number of securitizers who are SEC registrants announced losses resulting from downward adjustments to previously recorded retained interests in securitizations. The adjustments usually stemmed from securitized mortgage assets that prepaid more quickly than the seller's original estimates. The losses also led equity analysts to increasingly question the "quality of earnings" of many securitizers. The analysts pointed out that FAS 125 gains are, for the most part, non-cash; instead, the gains usually result from recording assets that represent an estimate of the present value of *future* cash flows.

In response, some securitizers indicated that they would utilize more conservative assumptions when calculating the gain or loss securitizations. More conservative assumptions mitigate or eliminate subsequent downward adjustments if adverse market developments occur.

Also, in at least one well publicized case, it was not clear that the securitizer would consistently apply assumptions. That is, it appeared that the securitizer might use more conservative assumptions for newly securitized assets but would not use similar assumptions when estimating the fair value of retained interests from previously securitized assets. Different assumptions should be used when warranted by the facts and circumstances of the specific assets securitized. For example, a securitizer is justified in making different estimates for loans with substantively different terms or economic characteristics.

These developments prompted the SEC staff to make an announcement at the March 1998 EITF meeting, codified as Topic D-69 in the *EITF Abstracts*. Key points contained in the announcement are as follows:

1. Recognition of gains or losses on the sale of financial assets is not elective.
2. In estimating the fair value of retained and new interests, the assumptions used in those valuations must be consistent with market conditions. Using assumptions that are not consistent with current market conditions in order to ascribe intentionally low or high values to new or retained interests is not appropriate.
3. Assumptions and methodologies used in estimating the fair value of similar instruments should be consistent. It would be inappropriate to use significantly different values or assumptions for new retained interests that are similar to existing retained interests.
4. Significant assumptions used in estimating the fair value of retained and new interests at the balance sheet date should be disclosed. Significant assumptions generally include quantitative amounts or rates of default, prepayment and interest.

Does FASB 125 Guide the
Separate Financial Statements of the SPE?

FASB 125 does not address the balance sheet accounting by the SPE, which is usually the registrant for SEC filing purposes, or related trusts. The various structures, though, may have implications for the form and content of audited financial statements which may be called for in 1934 Act filings. For pass-through certificate structures and for CMOs accounted for as sales, financial statements have typically been considered not applicable.

Can I Record an Asset for Servicing?

You may record an asset for servicing if the benefits of servicing are expected to be more than adequate compensation to service the assets. [13] This would best be evidenced by the ability to receive (as opposed to pay) cash up-front if the rights and obligations under the servicing contract were to be assigned to another servicer.

Servicing is inherent with financial assets; however, it only becomes a distinct asset when contractually separated from the underlying assets via a sale or securitization of the assets, with servicing retained. [35] A servicer of the assets commonly receives the benefits of servicing — revenues from contractually specified servicing fees, late charges, and other ancillary revenues, including "float" — and incurs the costs of servicing those assets. Typically, in securitizations, the benefits of servicing are not expected to be less than adequate compensation to the servicer. Adequate compensation is the amount of benefits of servicing that would fairly compensate a substitute servicer should one be required, which includes the profit that would be demanded in the marketplace. Adequate compensation is determined by the marketplace, it does not vary according to the specific servicing costs of the servicer. Therefore, a servicing contract that entitles the servicer to receive benefits of servicing just equal to adequate compensation, regardless of whether the servicer's own servicing costs are higher or lower, does not result in recognizing a servicing asset or servicing liability.

FASB 125 makes no distinction between "normal servicing fees" and "excess servicing fees." The distinction is between "contractually specified servicing fees" and rights to excess interest (IO strips). Contractually specified servicing fees are all amounts that, in the contract, are due the servicer, in exchange for servicing the assets. These fees would no longer be received by the original servicer if the beneficial owners of the serviced assets (or their trustees or agents) were to exercise their actual or potential authority, under the contract, to shift the servicing to another servicer. Depending on the servicing contract, those fees may include: a normal servicing fee, and some or all of the difference between the interest rate collectable on the asset being serviced and the rate to be paid to the beneficial owners of those assets. [243]

Consider the following example. Financial assets with a coupon rate of 10% are securitized. The pass-through rate to holders of the SPE's beneficial interests is 8%. The servicing contract entitles the seller-servicer to 100 basis points as servicing compensation. The seller is entitled to the remaining 100 basis points as excess interest. Adequate compensation to a successor servicer for these assets is assumed to be 75 basis points. Exhibit 5 depicts the arrangement.

Exhibit 5: Graphical Depiction of Excess Servicing Arrangement

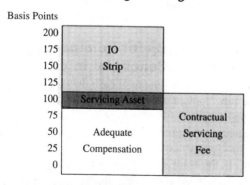

Servicing assets created in a securitization shall initially be measured at their allocated carrying amount, based upon the relative fair values at the date of securitization. Rights to future interest income from the serviced assets in amounts that exceed the contractually specified servicing fees should be accounted for separately from the servicing asset. Those amounts are not servicing assets — they are IO strips to be accounted for as described later. Servicing assets are to be amortized in proportion to, and over the period of, estimated net servicing income (the excess of servicing revenues over servicing costs). This is often referred to as the net income forecast or proportional method of amortization. If the estimated net servicing income in month 1 represents 1% of sum total on an undiscounted basis of the estimated net servicing income over the life of the pool, then 1% of the original asset recorded for servicing rights would be amortized as a reduction of servicing fee income in month 1. This is in contrast to a depletion method or liquidation method which is based on declining principal balances or number of loans. The servicing asset must be subsequently evaluated and measured for impairment as follows:

1. Stratify servicing assets based on one or more of the predominant risk characteristics of the underlying financial assets. Those characteristics may include financial asset type, size, interest rate, date of origination, term, and geographic location.
2. Recognize impairment through a valuation allowance for an individual stratum. The amount of impairment recognized shall be the amount by which the carrying amount of servicing assets for a stratum exceeds its fair value. The fair value of servicing assets that have not been recognized shall not be used in the evaluation of impairment.
3. Adjust the valuation allowance to reflect changes in the measurement of impairment subsequent to the initial measurement. Fair value in excess of the carrying amount for that stratum shall not be recognized. [37g]

Servicing is not a "financial asset" under FASB 125. Accordingly, there is a higher threshold analysis of "risks and rewards" to achieve sale accounting when mortgage servicing rights are transferred.[13]

Should I Record a Liability for Retained Credit Risk or is it Part of the Retained Beneficial Interest in the Asset?

The transferor should focus on the source of cash flows in the event of a claim by the trust. If the trust can only "look to" cash flows from the underlying financial assets, the transferor has retained a portion of the credit risk through its retained interest and a separate obligation should not be recorded. Credit losses from the underlying assets do affect, however, the measurement of the fair value of the transferor's retained interest.

In contrast, if the transferor could be obligated for more than the cash flows provided by its retained interest and, therefore, could be required to "write a

---

[13] See EITF Issues No. 90-21 and 95-5.

check" to reimburse the trust or others for credit related losses on the underlying assets, a separate liability should be recorded at fair value on the date of transfer.

How Will FASB 125 Affect Interest-Only Strips and Other Securities Subject to Prepayment Risk?

Interest-only strips, loans or other receivables that can be contractually prepaid or otherwise settled in such a way that the holder would not recover substantially all of its investment are to be carried at fair value, similar to investments in debt securities classified as available-for-sale or trading under FASB 115. [14] This will apply regardless of whether these assets were purchased or were retained in a securitization. Note that some of these assets (e.g. uncertificated interest strips) were not previously subject to FASB 115 because they did not meet the definition of a "security."

No guidance is given as to the size of a premium that would trigger this provision. However, the FASB staff has said that the probability of prepayment is not relevant in deciding whether this provision should apply. So, the potential for a loss of a portion of the investment would not be evaluated differently for a wideband PAC Class versus a Support Class. For those assets classified as available for sale, the write-down for the "other than temporary impairment" test specified in EITF 93-18 also applies. The 93-18 test calls for an income statement writedown to fair value, whenever the present value of the estimated future cash flows discounted at a risk-free rate is less than the amortized cost basis of the instrument. For those assets classified as trading, the impairment and measurement guidelines of 93-18 would not apply, since they are already marked to market in earnings.[14]

Exhibit 6 provides a comparison of contractual servicing asset versus IO strip accounting under FASB 125. The difference in accounting between servicing fees and IOs could lead seller-servicers to select a stated servicing fee that results in larger servicing assets and lower retained IO interests (or vice versa), with an eye to subsequent accounting. The potential accounting incentives for selecting a higher or lower stated servicing fee may counterbalance each other. On the other hand, because of this potential earnings volatility, many issuers may look to ways to sell or repackage servicing and IO strips.[15]

Are There Any Special Rules for Mortgage Bankers?

A mortgage banking enterprise does not have the same latitude as do other securitizers with respect to the classification of retained interests in a securitization of mortgage loans. Under FASB 125, a mortgage banker (i.e., an entity engaged in mortgage banking activities) was required to classify as *trading* (i.e., mark to market through earnings) all mortgage-backed securities retained after the securitization of mortgage loans held for sale. Retained mortgage-backed securities include senior and subordinated classes, interest-only strips and residuals.

---

[14] See discussion below about mortgage bankers.

[15] Note the transfer of servicing is covered in EITF Issues No. 90-21 and 95-5, not FASB 125.

Exhibit 6: Comparison of Contractual Servicing Asset versus IO Strip Accounting under FASB 125

	Servicing Asset	IO Strip Receivable
Definition	Amounts that, per contract, are due to the servicer for servicing, if more than adequate compensation	Entitlements to interest spread beyond the contractually specified servicing fee
Initial Recorded Amount	Allocated cost-Relative to FMV	Allocated cost-Relative to FMV
Adjusted Initial Recorded Amount	No adjustment	Adjustment up or down to FMV, through earnings, if trading, or equity, if available-for-sale
Income Recognition	Amortized in proportion to and over the period of estimated net servicing income	Trading: Marked to market Available-for-sale: Level yield, prospective adjustment under EITF 89-4
Balance Sheet Carrying Value	Allocated cost, less accumulated amortization and valuation allowance	Fair market value
Recognition of Impairment	Through valuation allowance for an individual strata when carrying amount exceeds fair value; change in valuation allowance in earnings	Trading: Marked to Market; AFS: Writedown to fair value under EITF 93-18 when yield is less than risk-free rate
Hedging Eligibility	Both are hedgeable risks; if an effective derivative can be found	
Income Taxes	As earned, if "reasonable"	Allocated cost-Relative to FMV; tax level yield method

Exhibit 7: Comparison of the Accounting for a Mortgage Banker Under the Exposure Draft to the Accounting Followed by Other Securities

	Holding Intent with Respect to Retained Interest	Is the Retained Interest a Security as Defined by FAS 115?	Classification Permitted for a Mortgage Banker	Classification Permitted for a Non-Mortgage Banker
1	To Sell	Yes	Trading	Trading, or Available for Sale
2	To Sell	No	Trading	No FASB standard applies. Generally, lower of cost or market*
3	Not to Sell	Yes	Trading, Available for Sale, or Held to Maturity*	Same
4	Not to Sell	No	Not covered by the Exposure Draft. Generally, amortized cost.*	No FASB standard applies. Generally, amortized cost.*

* If a retained interest (security or nonsecurity) bears a significant risk of loss due to prepayments (e.g., an I/O strip), it must be accounted for like a trading or an available for sale security.

In April 1998, the FASB issued for exposure a proposed standard that would more closely align, but not conform, the classification choices of a mortgage banker to the classification choices of other securitizers. Exhibit 7 compares the accounting for a mortgage banker under the exposure draft to the accounting followed by other securitizers.

If adopted, the new standard would be effective upon issuance. A mortgage banker has the option to reclassify from trading, mortgage backed securities (and other beneficial interests) retained after the securitization of mortgage loans held for sale based upon its present ability and intent to hold those investments (situation 3 in Exhibit 7). The mortgage banker must also reclassify certain other beneficial interests into the trading category (situation 2 in Exhibit 7). The latter situation triggers the recognition of any unrealized gain or loss at the date of the transfer.

What if We Put Humpty-Dumpty Back Together Again?

A "desecuritization" is the process by which securities created in a securitization are transformed back into their underlying loans or other financial assets. In EITF 90-2, a consensus had been reached that an investor should record an exchange of IO and PO securities of the same trust for the related mortgage-backed security, at fair value, at the date of the exchange, with gain or loss recognized on the exchange. Since FASB 125 does not allow sale treatment when an asset is exchanged for 100% of the beneficial interests in that asset; it seemed logical to the FASB staff that sale treatment should not be allowed for the opposite case of an exchange of all of the beneficial interests in the asset (e.g., senior and subordinated classes) for the asset itself (e.g., the mortgage loans). Accordingly, EITF 90-2 has been nullified.[16]

---

[16] See EITF Topic D-51, "The Applicability of FASB Statement No. 115 to Desecuritizations of Financial Assets."

Chapter 8

Technology Issues in Asset-Backed Securitization

James E. Myers
Marketing Manager
Lewtan Technologies, Inc.

INTRODUCTION

Why is technology an important part of the securitization process? Many of the reasons are no different from those in other financial service applications — large volumes of data processed in an environment where accuracy, auditability, and automation are of paramount importance. Asset securitization is a highly data-intensive endeavor with a set of diverse information and reporting needs.

However, other technological requirements are still unique to the securitization process. The very nature of establishing a special-purpose vehicle (SPV), which requires a new set of books to account for the sold receivables, is a financial innovation that encourages technology. With ever-changing structures, the permutations for investors are nearly boundless. To satisfy investor appetite for variety and maximum yields, any asset with an anticipated cash flow is a target for securitization. (For proof, just look at viatical settlements, future flows, and stranded utility costs.) Consequently, systems must be flexible, expandable, and continuously updated.

Compounding the difficulties surrounding ABS systems is the relative scarcity of systems knowledge among ABS professionals. Consider how many activities in an organization require interaction of participants from legal, accounting, operations, finance, and systems areas.

Typically, people who understand the structured-finance aspects of securitizations lack in-depth understanding of how a receivables accounting system accrues interest, allocates payments, or handles bounced checks. There is ample occasion for miscommunication, and all participants follow a learning curve as they gain understanding of other departmental functions and attempt to put systems in place.

Furthermore, with the considerable number of internal and external participants involved in a single ABS transaction, the hand-off of deal documents and actual data is extensive. Information passes through underwriters, lawyers, credit enhancers, rating agencies, investors, and issuers, among others. Many of these

137

players have sophisticated systems requirements to analyze, structure, and monitor the transaction from preclosing through cleanup call.

This chapter offers a primer for a subset of ABS systems and technology issues. It covers the following:

- Requirements of securitization participants over the transaction's life cycle.
- Some calculations of a securitized transaction that require servicing and accounting unrelated to an issuer's normal processing of the underlying assets.
- Details to cover when developing or selecting the appropriate securitization technology.
- Technical innovations available for modeling new ABS transactions or reverse-engineering existing deals.
- A prediction for the future of securitization technology.

TECHNOLOGY REQUIREMENTS OVER THE DEAL LIFE CYCLE

To understand fully the technology requirements for an ABS system, the needs of participants at each phase of a deal must be considered. This chapter considers the roles of issuer/servicer, underwriter, rating agency, credit enhancer, and investor.

Not considered here are other systems used in the originator's organization for credit scoring, primary servicing of the underlying asset, collections tracking for chargeoffs, and general ledger reporting, since each of those systems exists in the absence of securitization.

Similarly, the systems employed by the trustee for handling collections and tracking bondholder information are not considered here as they are the same as those used for other fixed-income products. Although asset-backed commercial paper conduits bring a unique set of systems requirements to bear, only the systems employed for term asset-backed deals will be discussed herein for the sake of clarity.

The technology requirements for securitization begin with the conceptualization of a deal, continue through the analysis and deal formation, and end with the ongoing servicing, accounting, and surveillance.

Exhibit 1 provides a bird's eye view of some technology requirements of major players in an asset-backed transaction.

Pool Selection

The process begins when the decision is made to examine ABS as a financing alternative. First, the assets under consideration are dissected and analyzed. Second, historical loss and prepayment experience are sought to provide a prediction for future cash-flow experience. Third, assets that will not pass rating agency and investor scrutiny are filtered out of the eligible asset pool. The remaining assets form the basis for the securitized pools.

Exhibit 1: Technology Checklist

	Conduit Sponsor	Issuer Servicer	Underwriter	Rating Agency	Credit Enhancer	Investor
Collateral Analysis	X	X	X		X	
Pool Selection	X	X	X			
Cash Flow Projections	X	X	X	X	X	X
Deal Structuring	X	X	X	X	X	
Receivables Purchase	X					
Point of Sale Reporting		X				
Collection Tracking	X	X				
Static Pool Analysis	X	X	X			
Average Daily Balance Calc.		X				
Asset/Liability Management	X					
Gain in Sale Computation		X				
Investor Reporting	X	X				
Surveillance	X	X	X	X	X	X
Investment Analysis						X
Cash Management	X					
Accounting	X	X				

Systems are required in this phase to provide the segregation of assets and to sort through the multifarious permutations of deal criteria. Geographic concentration limits, desired coupon rates to ensure sufficient excess spread, and minimum and maximum acceptable balances are all considered. Systems will assist in identifying the assets eligible for securitization.

When proceeding with a transaction, the analysis of the deal becomes more extensive. The issuer or underwriter continues to require systems for the analysis of the underlying collateral and for pool selection. Once the proposed pool of assets is selected, systems are required to create the stratifications and cross-tabulations of data that comprise the prospectus and rating agency reports. Point-of-sale reports detail the assets that have been selected. It is often important to have a procedure in place to tag the selected assets for removal from an issuer's balance sheet as well as to untag them — to return them to the books should the deal unwind before coming to market.

Static Pool Analysis

It is becoming more and more common to provide "static pool" or "vintage" reporting in addition to basic asset summary reports to the rating agencies when presenting a pool of assets for securitization. Static pool or vintage analysis involves unique requirements that are not met by most operational reports and systems.

A static-pool analysis helps reveal how delinquencies, losses, and prepayments develop over time. A critical question that the rating agencies and guarantors ask is: How will the fixed pool of assets being securitized perform over the life of the securitization? Looking at the performance of the entire portfolio (dynamic pool) does not help. The overall growth in total assets over time can easily mask trends in the older receivables. Looking at different static pools (vintages) helps show how the assets have performed over long periods of time.

Components
The components of a static-pool analysis illustrate why traditional "snapshot" reporting is insufficient to satisfy the rating agencies' requirements. The following steps create a typical static-pool analysis:

1. Break portfolio into vintages, typically quarterly (all originations during a particular quarter).
2. Prepare tables illustrating how each vintage performed month by month or quarter by quarter, from the point of the origination.
3. For each quarter, determine:
   - Beginning/ending number of loans in vintage still active.
   - Beginning/ending principal balance.
   - Amortization during period.
   - Prepayments during period.
   - Delinquencies in each category as of end of period.
   - Gross/net losses during period.

While these steps are easy to understand, there are many technological hurdles to clear.

Historical Data
The first hurdle in preparing a static pool analysis often arises in the availability and accessibility of historical data. Backup procedures can change over time along with specific hardware and software used to store data. Some companies may not maintain historical data for a period of time sufficient to develop significant reports (typically at least five years of historical data are requested). Additionally, the operational procedures in some institutions may create a situation in which accounts are eliminated from record after a year or so of inactivity, or the same account numbers may be reassigned after a given period of time. Such occurrences make the technological challenges of static-pool reporting as much an art as a science.

Interpretation
Interpreting and analyzing the data from historical backup present the second difficulty in developing static pool reports. Provided that the data can be accessed successfully, there can be multiple systems involved and consequently multiple data retrievals for even the same historical point in time. Operational methods may have changed over time. Even the underlying receivable accounting system may have been converted, added to, or otherwise modified over the historical period in question.

Deal Modeling

Intricate modeling systems are required by various parties before a deal goes to market. Stress tests are performed for a variety of bond structures to identify which circumstances will produce shortfalls to the various classes of investors.

Essential deal-structuring functions include the ability to size tranches, generate price/yield tables, model complex trigger events that could alter the payout sequence of the bonds, and manipulate credit enhancement and other deal features. The capacity to modify quickly and easily the prepayment, default, delinquency, and recovery assumptions for the underlying collateral is also important.

Servicing

Once the securitization has closed, the servicer's reporting to the trust becomes the ongoing systems concern. Servicing for a securitization requires the translation of asset-related information into investor-related information. For most asset classes, recording the appropriate values on the servicer's certificate or settlement statement will dictate calculations to be made at the asset level. A system that reconciles every output that the investor views back to the account level will provide assurance for auditors, rating agencies, and investors.

Flexibility

A securitization tracking system should also be flexible. As many issuers intend to come to market more than once, the ability to create different calculations and bond payout hierarchies is critical. A securitization system will ideally support all accrual and asset types in an issuer's portfolio to ensure that the system's capabilities do not limit an organization's financing objectives.

Independence

Because a securitization system is independent of a receivable accounting system, the ability to track all issuances on a single system simplifies the ongoing reporting task. Independence of an issuer's primary receivable accounting system is important to ensure that securitization reports can be generated in a timely manner. Moreover, there are many securitization-specific calculations that mandate the maintenance of separate fields in the system to house securitization values that do not exist on most receivable accounting systems.

Interface with General Ledger

A securitization system should have the ability to interface with the issuer's general ledger. While many organizations are able to tag and segregate accounts through a subledger balance, other issuers prefer to tag the accounts through a separate securitization system and employ contra-accounts to remove the assets and associated income from their books. In the most sophisticated systems, a user has the automatic ability to repurchase receivables that violate the representations and warranties of the deal rather than requiring separate "exception" checks and ad hoc reports. Regardless of the accounting methods chosen, securitization requires the maintenance of a new set of books for the SPV.

Surveillance

After the deal closes, the same parties must keep an eye on the performance of the deal via systems. An increase in delinquencies has heightened market sensitivity to the investigation of default scenarios. As delinquencies increase, so does the need for surveillance. Any threat of an economic downturn on the horizon increases this need. Today's market offers a prevalence of lower-quality asset securitizations (B and C auto paper was the largest asset class by dollar volume in second-quarter 1996). This tendency brings an ever-present need to monitor new asset types to justify better pricing in subsequent deals. All of these factors signal the importance of systemic, regular surveillance.

The systems that exist to monitor an ABS deal begin with the originator's own internal portfolio management reporting and continue through the investor's portfolio management systems. Issuers demand a streamlined, intuitive surveillance software that performs functions the issuers are hard-pressed to perform on their own. Some examples are:

- Sophisticated trend analysis.
- Automated tracking and re-valuation of the gain on sale.
- Early-warning tools or ticklers that would automate deal triggers and identify actions the issuer could take to salvage a deal from a negative trend in collateral performance.

Investors that actively monitor their ABS deals require:

- Accurate, timely security pricing to evaluate performance.
- Standard interfaces to their portfolio management systems.
- The ability to track senior and subordinated pieces.
- The ability to mark their portfolios to market.
- Reprojection capability to reevaluate the underlying deal from time to time.

Rating agencies rely on the quality of data, speed, access of data for their analysts, flexibility to adapt to future market changes, and an automated, systematic approach to surveillance to minimize costs. Credit enhancers benefit from surveillance in many of the same ways as rating agencies but also require a system that can project fees, forecast revenues, and determine whether reserve balances should be adjusted. An underwriter's trading and sales support functions require a high-performance processing server for instantaneous response time. An underwriter relies on systems for the pricing it provides to investors on a regular basis and for reengineering cash flows. Thus, ABS systems impact all parties in a securitized transaction.

SECURITIZATION SYSTEMS
VERSUS RECEIVABLE ACCOUNTING SYSTEMS

Asset-backed securitization introduces calculations, reporting requirements, and operational processes for the servicer that do not otherwise exist. In the nonsecuritized world, a receivable accounting system is used to track asset information such as payment history, balances, special statuses (such as nonaccruals, foreclosures, or bankruptcies), rate information, and other variables that detail the terms and performance of the assets. When a securitization is issued, the same asset servicing requirements exist, but a whole new set of variables must be tracked as well. A securitization system must calculate and store values at two levels:

- Asset level, to produce the calculations that are required for securitization of certain asset types. When aggregated, these asset-level variables typically comprise trust-level values.
- Trust level, to track all of the balances, statistics, and other information created by the securitization such as reserve fund balances, certificate balances for the different investor tranches, coupon rates, and scheduled interest for the bond classes.

As it is usually the servicer's goal to keep the obligor unaware that his or her particular receivable has been securitized, the underlying receivable accounting system must continue processing as in the absence of securitization and the securitization system must provide the rest of the information needed for the deal.

Asset-Level Calculations

To best illustrate the types of asset-level calculations that are required of an ABS servicing system, consider a bank that has performed a securitization of auto loans. Suppose the bank has originated assets in several states and has a variety of accrual types including simple interest, actuarial, and Rule of 78s. Imagine the bank has force-placed insurance on some of these loans. Also, the bank may have set up a variety of dealer plans and is tracking the dealer reserve amounts, as well. For simplicity, our example has the bank issuing into a grantor trust.

This situation introduces some accounting and regulatory reporting challenges that the bank's securitization systems must address. If the bank achieves true sale treatment, the assets must be removed from the bank's balance sheet. Contra-accounting can be performed when the assets are segregated. On an ongoing basis, new force-placed insurance must be split from the sold loan amount, introducing split-balance accounting; a grantor trust does not allow for the addition of assets subsequent to closing. If the issuer offers a payment extension to one of the obligors to a date that extends beyond the securitization's stated legal maturity date, that loan must be repurchased and added back on to the seller's books. Of course, the securitization-specific accounting for the excess servicing income, servicer advance balances, and related items must also be established and maintained in a system. The average daily balance reported to the Office of the Comptroller of the Currency must reflect a mean that does not include the sold loans.

Meaningful Differences

Some calculations have meaning only when a loan has been securitized. For a public auto securitization, the balances carried on a servicer's books are different from that loan's pool balance to the securitization. Even in the case of a simple interest loan, events such as small credit balances, force-placed insurance additions, or defaults through delinquency (where the securitization may have a defined number of days before a loan must be defaulted to the investor even though the loan may not have been charged off on the seller's books) can leave that loan's contribution to the total securitized balance far different from the balance it would carry if not securitized. Even the actuarial and Rule of 78s accrual types, which are typically sold on a scheduled basis, will have far different book versus securitization balances.

Additionally, a servicer must track how much has been advanced on a particular delinquent loan, because if that loan defaults, the servicer is entitled to recoup any prior advances. Rule of 78s or actuarial loans that have paid in advance of schedule may be put into the trust's payahead account. Compensating interest, yield supplement amounts, pre-cutoff accrued interest, and other accruals are all based on a balance that does not exist on the underlying loan accounting system.

Benefits of Independent Processing

Even asset classes that do not require new calculations at the asset level for securitization (such as trade receivables or credit cards) benefit from the independent processing of a securitization servicing system. Static pool reporting dictates tracking receivable-level information. Home equity lines of credit require tracking new draws separately from sold portions. Leases can have a variety of payment schedules, residual treatments, and other nuances. Commercial mortgages have such unique contracts that reviewing each account's performance is mandatory. The list goes on and on.

Aggregation

Statistics and other information must be aggregated for the investor reports, for example: delinquencies, repossessions, bankruptcies, chargeoffs, weighted average coupons, weighted average remaining terms, and the number of active loans in the pool.

Trust-Level Calculations

We must next consider the servicing of trust-level information. The pooling of assets into a security introduces the need for systems to track the liability side as well as the assets that support them. Maintaining the balances for the credit enhancement, calculating the amounts due to investors and other parties, and rolling that information forward from month to month are major functions of the securitization system.

The most sophisticated securitization system will automate the entire process. From automatically repurchasing receivables that violate the representations and warranties of the deal to rebooking any remaining assets for the cleanup call, the securitization system performs functions unique to the ABS world.

BACK-OFFICE TECHNOLOGY: BUY VERSUS BUILD

A key strategic decision is whether to purchase software that is readily available on the market or to build software in-house. For repeat issuers or conduit sponsors, the cost of building and maintaining a system may be far greater than the cost of outsourcing that responsibility. The deal parameters are often changing up to the last minute, and the systems development time schedule is independent of market conditions that may impact when to bring the deal to market. Combined with the dissimilar agendas of various internal departments, building a system is a difficult task.

Project Team Competition

When making a buy-versus-build decision, consider the organization's ability to adapt to changing requirements. Have members of the project team already worked on similar projects? Have they ever worked together? Is there a strong project manager with securitization experience? Change must be managed both at the beginning of the project and through the life of the deal. The underwriter and rating agencies call for changes in pool composition and format for investor reports. The deal could be postponed if the market conditions are not right. Does the issuer have the ability to tag the sold receivables and then untag them should the deal unwind? What other projects are competing for the time of the securitization team members?

Ongoing Operating Costs

Ongoing costs of operating a system should also be considered when weighing the decision of a software purchase. Software providers typically invest tens of thousands of hours per year in updating their products to remain current with the industry and available technology. In-house systems can quickly become obsolete if the market changes. Moreover, they are often rendered useless if an issuer wishes to expand into a new asset class. Supporting variations from deal to deal, maintaining the ability to securitize a large portion of a portfolio, adapting to regulatory changes, and keeping pace with modifications to the underlying receivable accounting system are all considerations that must be assessed in line with a potential software purchaser's anticipated securitization plans.

The bottom line is that vendor-supported systems must provide the necessary reduction in operating expenses to mandate purchase. In addition to rewriting or scrapping old systems, there are many questions to be answered even if plans call for issuing only a single deal. How much staff time is required to produce the necessary reports? How much staff time is required to generate the accounting entries? How much incremental staff time does it take to support additional deals? Does the issuer's securitization servicing system preclude launching a new deal fast enough to take advantage of opportune market conditions?

Quality of Output

There is no room for compromise on quality of the system's output. Does the system provide a strictly controlled environment with comprehensive audit trails? Can the entries on investor reports be reconciled with detailed asset level information? How much re-keying of information is required, and what risks does that create? Will the annual audit fare well? If the staff that developed this system moves to other departments, can the system still be supported and/or modified?

The output of the securitization servicing system reflects the competence of an organization to the outside world. Therefore, there should be no compromise when investing in the back-office operations that will make the overall securitization as profitable as anticipated.

FRONT-OFFICE: FINDING THE RIGHT MODELING ENVIRONMENT

For underwriters, investors, rating agencies, credit enhancers, issuers, and any other party wishing to analyze a deal, the ability to model complicated ABS deal structures is important. The only party that may not employ a structuring model to analyze a deal is an investor purchasing senior tranches for which the underlying credit enhancement has decreased the need for sophisticated analytics. In that case, purchases are made based solely on triple-A ratings. But for all other parties, structuring tools are used from a deal's inception through its entire life cycle.

Scenario Analysis

Structuring systems feature the ability to analyze cash flows in a variety of deal structures. The ability to run multiple cash-flow scenario analyses is essential for stress-testing the structure of the deal, sizing the tranches, and pricing. At the most basic level, a user should have the ability to use the standard industry prepayment models (CPR, ABS, SMM, etc.), vary the prepayment speeds, loss and recovery amounts and timing, and delinquency assumptions, among other variables.

More sophisticated systems will allow for modeling sophisticated cash-flow "waterfalls" to multiple tranches, credit enhancement types, and fees. Standard system reports depicting the amortization of each tranche and general statistics such as duration, yield to maturity, convexity, and a price/yield table will significantly reduce an analyst's time in reviewing the output.

Reusability

The reusability of the model is also important. The servicer will require a model for analyzing the anticipated excess servicing fee and for the reprojection of the deal in midlife for the purposes of repricing or adjusting the gain on sale.

Selecting Options

The market for vendor-supported systems for securitization structuring is filled with many participants, unlike the market for any other type of securitization software. In addition to off-the-shelf products, many underwriters have developed in-house, proprietary models. For those who do not use securitization-specific software, spreadsheets are most often the tool of choice. With many options to choose from, how does someone wishing to structure or reverse-engineer an existing deal know what to use? This section discusses the pros and cons of each approach while delineating the basic environments of the vendor-supported systems.

Collateral Capability

Prior to modeling the features of the bond, there are systems requirements surrounding the selection of eligible receivables. Securitization functionality at this stage must allow for assets to be filtered out that do not meet restrictive covenants of a deal. Occasionally, purchasing additional assets that would otherwise make the eligible pool is disallowed due to the increased concentration risk introduced by selecting too many assets with similar characteristics. A robust system has the ability to segregate eligible assets, analyze the performance of those assets both historically and on a forecasted basis, and produce the necessary stratification and cross-tabular reports as needed for a prospectus.

Spreadsheets Versus Vendor-Supported Software

There are many advantages to using a spreadsheet to model an ABS transaction. Spreadsheets are flexible and easy to use. They are relatively inexpensive in terms of upfront, hard-dollar costs compared with the cost of a system designed specifically for securitization. Most people in the financial arena are familiar with spreadsheets and have them readily accessible. Moreover, the output from a spreadsheet model can be used to create attractive reports, graphs, and exhibits.

The disadvantages of a spreadsheet environment may not be as apparent. Spreadsheets offer limited functionality. They were designed for multiple purposes — from maintaining accounting reports to creating graphs to acting as a database application. Securitization-specific software can provide better avenues to communicate the structure of an asset-backed deal once it is modeled. Moreover, a spreadsheet lacks the conveniences of off-the-shelf software. Spreadsheets are not auditable. A stand-alone system, on the other hand, will offer the ability to "freeze" a model once a user decides the model is stable (that is, when the deal has closed). Spreadsheet models are unwieldy with complexity. Often, the person who originally modeled the deal must be present to explain what a spreadsheet is doing. When that person moves on to another deal, he or she may not be able to recall how the old model performed. Finally, a spreadsheet will typically perform much more slowly for a sophisticated deal structure, making it prohibitive in environments that demand a broad scenario analysis. The sum of these all-in costs makes spreadsheets a more expensive alternative for many.

Vendor Software

Up to this point, we have not differentiated the many types of vendor software available. These variations can result in more or less end-user functionality but, in most cases, the biggest difference is in the philosophical approach to deal modeling. The structuring software on the market today has one or more of three basic characteristics: table-driven tools, script-based languages, and object-based environments. The pros and cons of each are discussed below.

Table Driven When a structuring tool houses a data base of tranches, prepayment models, and other variables, it can often model simple deals with ease. One problem with a table-driven system for the securitization market, however, is that deal nuances and new deal structures are constantly emerging. Consequently, the data base of user options may not contain the right deal feature until after that feature has been introduced to the market and incorporated into the software. Alternatively, a new deal structure may result in a change to the fundamental relationship between the elements in multiple tables, rendering the system obsolete for cutting-edge transactions or as structural innovations emerge.

Script-Based These products offer a greater range of flexibility than table-driven modeling tools. However, what they make up for in flexibility they typically lose in ease of use. Often a program is designed in C++ or an equivalent programming language that requires a programmer to construct the deal's payout waterfall. As discussed earlier in this chapter, it is rare to find many individuals who possess both a thorough understanding of ABS and an accomplished programming skill set.

Object-Based Structuring tools that are object-based offer the best of both worlds. While a pallette of standard objects can be found to provide all of the deal features that could otherwise be stored in a data base, this type of product utilizes an open environment to allow for users to create new deal elements as they model. As seen in Exhibit 2, the object-based product has an additional advantage: the flow of funds through the deal is depicted visually, allowing for better communication among parties on how the deal is constructed. The disadvantage to this modeling tool is its newness. While the other types of software have a user base that has made progress up the learning curve, object-based software is not typical in other financial service applications.

Exhibit 2: An Object-Based Structuring Tool

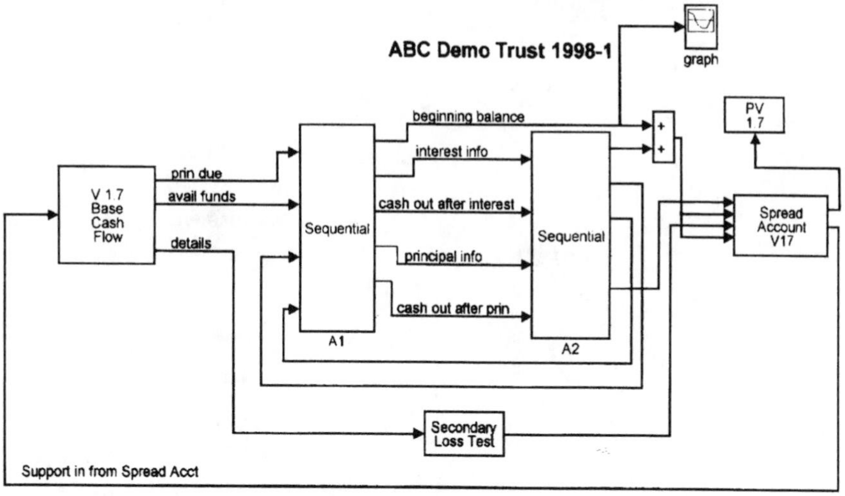

ABC Demo Trust 1998-1

FUTURE TECHNOLOGY DIRECTION IN ABS

What does the future hold for securitization technology? As stated earlier in this chapter, securitization is a highly data-intensive industry. It employs complex, innovative, financial structures. Today's hot new software can rapidly become tomorrow's legacy system. As securitization continues to expand into new asset classes and into international arenas, collateral-tracking, bond-tracking, and deal-structuring software will follow.

For ABS deals backed by commodity-type assets, market efficiency will demand a standardization of data elements describing each deal. Systems that house these asset classes will undergo a process of data normalization as the industry begins to adopt the data standard. The systems currently in place will undergo revisions to simplify the exchange of data among deal participants.

In the end, technology makes the exchange of data and information more efficient and automated.

Chapter 9

The Role of the Trustee in Asset-Backed Securitization

Karen Cook
Assistant Vice President
Bankers Trust Company

F. Jim Della Sala
Principal
Bankers Trust Company

INTRODUCTION

The role of the trustee originated during the early years of the mortgage loan industry's development and evolved out of the need for an individual to represent the collective interests of investors who held direct interests in defaulted or foreclosed mortgages. A bank was appointed as trustee for a bond issued under a trust indenture for the first time in 1839. Although the duties of the trustee were minimal, the benefits to naming an institution, rather than an individual, as trustee was a significant step in the development and expansion of the functions of the trustee.

As transactions became more complex and more first-time issuers entered the marketplace, the number of defaulted bonds in the industry increased. The role of the trustee adapted to these changes by assuming additional responsibilities under the trust indenture. This empowered the trustee to better protect the interests of bondholders in default scenarios. Institutions offering corporate trust services found it necessary to create separate corporate trust departments within their organization and to more carefully evaluate their responsibilities as a trustee. As a result, standard policies and business practices were developed to protect their own interests as well. The SEC passed the Trust Indenture Act of 1939, which defines the eligibility requirements for a trustee and guidelines on the standard conduct of a trustee.[1]

Many different types of trustees exist in the asset-backed industry. They can be broadly categorized as indenture, owner, off-shore, and successor. The role of trustees are basically the same for all trustee types. The main responsibility of the trustee is to represent the interest of the securityholders, particularly during an

---

[1] Robert I. Landau, *Corporate Trust Administration and Management, 4th Ed.* (New York: Columbia University Press, 1992), pp. 51-54.

event of default. Other responsibilities of the trustee include monitoring covenant compliance, authentication of the asset-backed securities, and enforcement of remedies during an event of default as defined in the governing documents.

"TYPES" OF TRUSTEES

Indenture Trustee

Some of the administrative functions of the indenture trustee include monitoring the cash flow, account reconciliation, investment of funds held in trust accounts, custody of securities for the benefit of securityholders, holding security interest in the assets, and payment of principal, interest and trust expenses on the distribution date.

The trustee should monitor the transaction proactively throughout the life of the transaction. The trustee receives periodic reports from the servicer which detail principal paydown, collections, defaults, and delinquencies of the receivables pool. By reviewing these reports, the trustee can identify potential trigger events or servicer defaults. The trustee evaluates whether the form of the reports and opinions required to be delivered by the other parties to the transaction conform to the requirements of the governing documents. These governing documents also specify how a trustee should proceed after being notified of any triggers or events of default.

Owner Trustee

An owner trustee holds legal title to the owner trust estate which includes funds on deposit in trust accounts and all other property of the trust. The owner trustee represents the interest of certificateholders who own trust certificates evidencing their beneficial interest to the trust estate. In an owner trust structure, the indenture trustee represents the beneficial interests of the noteholders and retains the typical duties of an indenture trustee pursuant to the trust indenture.

Off-Shore Trustee

The appointment of an off-shore trustee is most common in cross border securitizations originated by issuers located in countries within Latin America, Europe or Asia. A special purpose entity, which purchases the assets for the receivables pool and issues the asset-backed securities, is established in an off-shore location such as the Cayman or Jersey Islands. The transaction documents are generally governed under the local trust law (where the trust is established). Collections generated from the receivables are deposited in off-shore trust accounts which are held by the off-shore trustee much like an indenture trustee. The off-shore trustee receives and invests funds and makes periodic disbursements as directed by the servicer.

An institution must meet specific qualifications in order to become an off-shore trustee. The requirements varies for each off-shore location; however, a corporate trust office must be established within the country's jurisdiction in order to receive local corporate trust powers.

Successor Trustee

A successor trustee is appointed if the original trustee either resigns or is removed from a transaction. The successor trustee inherits the same duties and responsibilities as the original trustee named in the documents. The successor trustee must coordinate with the departing trustee to transfer trust accounts, notify the securityholders, and coordinate with the servicer and depository of any revisions to instructions pertaining to collections and distributions.

AGENCY APPOINTMENTS

The appointment as trustee is typically packaged with related agency appointments of registrar, paying agent, and successor servicer. In addition, because of the sophisticated nature of asset-backed securities, the trustee is often asked to perform "non-traditional" roles in order to increase the marketability of the securities. These enhanced agency roles include calculation agent, document custodian, tax reporting agent, and back-up servicer.

Registrar

The primary responsibility of the registrar is to maintain a current record of registered securityholders and to process exchanges and registrations of transfers. Unlike the expanding role of the trustee in asset-backed transactions, the day-to-day responsibilities of the registrar have decreased over time. This is a result of the increased issuance of (fully registered) book-entry certificates instead of physical certificates. For book-entry issues, the securities are registered as a global certificate in the nominee name of the depository (i.e., Cede & Co. for The Depository Trust Company), and the registrar treats the nominee as the sole registered holder. The depository maintains the records of the participants and their corresponding holdings of the asset-backed securities. The depository is also responsible for sending notices and copies of servicer reports to investors and for effecting certificate or position transfers.

Paying Agent

A few days prior to the distribution date, the paying agent receives a servicer report from the servicer specifying the payment instructions for the distribution date. Either on or prior to the distribution date, the paying agent receives the full distribution amount from the servicer. On the distribution date, principal and interest payments to securityholders and other disbursements are made by the paying agent.

As with the role of the registrar, the role of the paying agent has narrowed in scope with the widespread issuance of (fully registered) book-entry certificates. On each distribution date, the entire principal and interest distribution amount is sent (via fedwire) by the paying agent to the depository for further distribution to the ultimate beneficial holders of the asset-backed securities.

Successor or Back-Up Servicer

A primary duty of the trustee is to assume the role of successor servicer in the event that the original servicer is removed or terminated.[2] The trustee is most likely to be required to step in as the successor servicer if there is an event of servicer default and subsequent termination and removal of the servicer. The successor servicer ensures that collections and other cash flows remain uninterrupted and that distributions continue to be paid to securityholders.

Some asset-backed transactions designate a separate entity in the governing documents, usually the trustee, as the back-up servicer. These types of situations generally arise for asset-backed transactions in which the issuer or servicer has a low credit rating or for transactions securitizing new or unique asset types. An additional level of monitoring of the servicer may be required in order for the transaction to obtain an investment grade rating.

Usually, the back-up servicer assumes the responsibility of reviewing and reverifying calculations on the servicer report. Prior to a servicer termination event, the back-up servicer may also run parallel reporting along with the existing servicer. The back-up servicer may also receive tapes from the servicer on a monthly basis and recalculate specific data contained in the servicer reports. The back-up servicer must be ready to immediately assume the role of the servicer should it become necessary.

The essential requirements for a back-up servicer include sophisticated systems, collection expertise, and an analytical staff to fulfill the servicing duties. The back-up servicer should examine the servicer's collection and reporting system for compatibility with its own internal asset servicing system. The back-up servicer should develop a plan for the migration of the receivable information onto its asset servicing system as well as determining how to monitor and manage ongoing contractual trigger events. The back-up servicer should schedule periodic on-site reviews of servicing facilities. It also must review the cash management procedures in regard to the asset collection and lockbox processing.

The trustee should identify any servicer advancing responsibilities for delinquent payments on the receivables or for the repurchase of non-conforming receivables and should evaluate any credit issues or conflicts which might arise with these advancing responsibilities. In some instances, where advancing is a requirement under the pooling and servicing agreement, the servicer or issuer is required to establish a reserve account with the trustee on the closing date and maintain a specified reserve balance for the duration of the transaction.

In certain situations, where the successor or back-up servicer is unable to fulfill all or part of the administrative and/or operational requirements internally, it may engage the services of a third-party vendor. The appointment of a third-party vendor does not replace the successor or back-up servicer's liability or contractual obligations on the transaction; however, through the engagement of a third-party vendor, some or all of the relevant administrative duties can be outsourced.

---

[2] The successor servicer is also known as "servicer of last resort".

Oftentimes, for a revolving asset type, an event of servicer termination will trigger the liquidation of the assets in the receivables pool and the final distribution payment to securityholders. Although this may not preclude the trustee from having to step in as successor servicer, it may eliminate some of the servicing, collection, and advancing responsibilities.

The appointment of a successor or back-up servicer on an asset-backed transaction adds value to the transaction by providing assurances to the rating agencies and investors that the collections and application of funds will continue uninterrupted regardless of economic distress of the servicer. Obviously, every attempt is made by the original servicer to avoid its removal from the transaction. The repercussions to the servicer of being terminated would include, but certainly not be limited to, a rating downgrade and a negative implication on the issuer's reputation in the asset-backed industry.

Document Custodian

A document custodian holds custody documents which typically represent the ownership interest in the underlying assets. These documents may be tangible assets such as notes, mortgages, and/or titles relating to the sale of assets to the trust or intangible assets such as collateral held in trust accounts (i.e., a letter of credit) which may be part of the credit enhancement for the transaction.

The custodian is often required to perform an initial review of the files to verify that certain documents are located in the files and to certify that information on the documents correspond to a master list description. The custodian, however, will not attest to the authenticity of the documents within the files. The custodian will also add trailing documents to files to cure exceptions, release files upon request, and provide periodic reports relating to the assets held in custody.

For warehouse lines, the role of the custodian may be enhanced to include cash management (account maintenance, wire transfers, and investments) for fundings and/or settlements, borrowing base calculation, and additional on-line reporting services.

Calculation Agent

The calculation agent receives collateral data from the servicer in a computer readable format. The data is validated by applying either basic or enhanced due diligence criteria, and is aggregated according to the specific transaction's requirements. Structured cash flow projection models are then used to periodically calculate and produce reports that describe distribution amounts to the various classes of securities issued within the transaction.

Tax Reporting Agent

The tax reporting agent ensures that annual tax returns are prepared and filed for the special purpose entity or trust issuing the asset-backed securities. Additionally, the tax reporting agent calculates any reportable original issue discount or premium on the asset pool in accordance with provisions of the Internal Revenue Code, as well as prepare, sign, and file the federal and state tax returns and all related schedules.

TRUSTEE'S ROLE IN THE LIFE OF AN ABS TRANSACTION

Pre-Closing

Upon appointment as trustee on an asset-backed transaction, the trustee receives (usually from the issuer's counsel) draft copies of the governing documents with related exhibits and the term sheet. The trustee's primary focus is to determine its specific duties and responsibilities for the asset-backed transaction. The trustee engages the services of either external or in-house counsel to review the legal aspects and risks associated with the trustee appointment.

When reviewing the governing documents, the trustee focuses on sections of the documents relating to the mechanics of the transaction, its duties, language relating to the perfection of security interest in the collateral, representations and warranties, incumbency language, indemnification and gross negligence (exculpatory) clauses, and event of default triggers and remedies. The trustee will review the events that would trigger the removal of the servicer, how the securityholders are notified, and the timing and procedures to step in as successor servicer. The trustee will also evaluate the servicing fee to ensure that it would be appropriately compensated for its services, should it become the successor servicer.

Numerous trust accounts need to be set-up by the trustee prior to closing. At the very least, collection and distribution accounts are required. All trust accounts for the transaction are registered in the name of the trustee for the benefit of the securityholders. Depending upon the transaction structure, a reserve account and/or collateral account may also be established and maintained by the trustee.

The servicer will open one or more lockbox accounts for the daily or periodic receipt of collections generated from the receivables. Although these accounts are maintained and operated by the servicer, these accounts are also registered in the name of the trustee and the trustee has the right, upon a servicer termination event, to direct the lockbox account provider to terminate the servicer's access to these accounts.

As part of its internal approval process, the trustee may conduct an internal credit review of the issuer and servicer before accepting an appointment as trustee. The review process typically includes reviewing financials of the servicer and issuer, their operating and management structure, company history, and operational capability.

If successor or back-up servicing is required, the trustee determines its ability to service assets in-house or its need to outsource the servicing to a third-party vendor. Also, as part of the servicing review, the trustee evaluates its own systems compatibility with the servicer's systems. The trustee may request an on-site due diligence tour of the servicing operations.

Closing

At closing, the trustee authenticates and delivers securities, executes the governing documents, and delivers the Trustee Certificate. The trustee also receives the initial funding into the trust accounts, which represents proceeds from the sale of the asset-backed securities to investors. An incumbency certificate from the issuer identifies the officers of the company who are authorized to direct the trustee to make investments and transfer funds held in trust accounts.

Post-Closing

The trustee is responsible for the periodic receipt of funds from the servicer which represent collections generated from the receivables. The servicer notifies the trustee of the amount which is to be deposited into each trust account and provides the trustee with investment instructions for the trust account balances. The eligible investments section of the governing documents defines the permitted investments for the trust funds.

Prior to each distribution date, the servicer sends the trustee a servicing report instructing the trustee of the disbursements to be made on the distribution date. The trustee may be responsible for providing copies of the servicing report to the securityholders, rating agencies, and credit enhancement providers. On each payment date, the trustee makes principal and interest payments to securityholders and pays servicing and other miscellaneous fees related to the transaction as specified in the servicer report.

Deal Defaults

If the trustee is notified of or obtains actual knowledge of a trigger event or an event of default, the governing documents specify the required steps to be taken. The bankruptcy or insolvency of the issuer or servicer are typical events which may result in an event of default. Furthermore, this may trigger a downgrading of the asset-backed security.

A possible repercussion from an event of default is the removal of the servicer. The trustee must be prepared to take over the servicing responsibilities which would include taking over the collection process. A trigger event may trigger the liquidation of assets and/or the amortization of notes. Should there be bankruptcy proceedings, the trustee's primary responsibility is to represent the beneficial interests of the securityholders and protect the "true sale" nature of the receivables.

Deal Termination

Generally, a provision in the governing documents allows for a "clean-up" call on the remaining principal balance of securities when the principal amount outstanding falls below a specified threshold of the original issuance amount.[3] The issuer will notify the trustee of the details regarding the final distribution date, including the

---

[3] Usually this is 10% of the original principal balance.

final distribution amount, the payment of fees and expenses and the transfer of interest on remaining assets, receivables, investments, and cash. The trustee will notify the securityholders of the final distribution date and the final distribution amount.

TRUSTEE RISKS

Inherent to any business arrangement is the risk to the parties involved in the transaction. Other than the investor, the trustee on an asset-backed securitization is subject to the most amount of risk. There are three different types of risks for the trustee: servicer non-performance, faulty transaction structure, and operational errors.

Servicer Non-Performance

After an asset-backed securitization closes, the trustee and the servicer of the assets are normally the only entities that retain any ongoing contractual duties. The trustee's day-to-day duties are dependent on getting timely and accurate information from the servicer. Additionally, the trustee may ultimately become the successor servicer if the existing servicer defaults on its contractual responsibilities.

Timely and Accurate Reporting of the Servicer
The trustee on an asset-backed securitization is responsible for taking direction from authorized individuals of the servicer for the investments and distributions made by the trustee. The operational timeframes in the transactions are structured very tightly to minimize the time between payments on the underlying assets and the principal and interest distributions to the securityholders. The trustee is reliant on the servicer for providing underlying asset payment information and determining distribution amounts to be paid on the next succeeding distribution date. If the servicer does not get the distribution information to the trustee in the designated timeframe, the trustee may not be able to make payments to the securityholders on the expected distribution date. Since the securityholders generally associate late payments as a "trustee problem," potential for future business for the trustee could be affected.

With asset-backed securitizations that are structured with a revolving period, the servicer is continuously[4] authorizing the trustee to transfer funds from the collection account to the asset funding account. Even in amortizing transactions, the trustee receives payment directions at least monthly. If the trustee receives erroneous directions, funds may be disbursed incorrectly. The trustee, after receiving notification of an incorrect payment direction by the servicer, is responsible for correcting the mistake. A servicer that continuously makes mistakes in its payment directions to the trustee will create additional work for the trustee which may cause the transaction to become unprofitable.

---

[4] In credit card transactions it is common for there to be daily funding, which are directed by the servicer.

Successor Servicing

A major risk to which the trustee is exposed is the risk that a servicer termination event occurs. This may require the trustee to assume the role of primary servicer. Asset-backed securitizations typically prohibit resignation by the servicer. When the role of servicing the assets is transferred to the trustee or a successor servicer, the portfolio is typically underperforming, servicing records are incomplete, and significant operational remediation is required.

The trustee may confront a situation which the original servicing fees no longer cover the expenses incurred for servicing the portfolio adequately.[5] Unless cash reserves or additional servicing fees exist in the transaction, the trustee may be required to cover the servicing fee shortfall in the transaction. If advancing on delinquent accounts is required of the servicer, the successor servicer, may lack the appetite for exposing its own capital for the benefit of the securityholders. The trustee may choose to delay the transfer of servicing until the remaining transaction participants (securityholders, bond insurer, and possibly the issuer/servicer) agree to cover all servicing fee shortfalls and servicer advances.

If the trustee does not have the internal expertise or infrastructure to service the assets in the transaction, it may hire a third-party servicer to service the assets. A third-party servicer may also be hired because the trustee does not have the proper legal or regulatory authorization in the location (state, county or city) of the obligor to service the assets. Thorough due diligence of the third-party servicer is very important in selecting the successor servicer by the trustee. The trustee's responsibility and liability, as named successor or back-up servicer, is normally not subrogated if a third-party entity is hired.

Faulty Transaction Structure

The transaction structure of an asset-backed securitization must be legally sound and must adequately distinguish the duties and responsibilities of each of the transaction parties in a clear and logical manner. If the legality of the transaction is challenged by any individual or governing authority, such as a Bankruptcy Court, the trustee must defend the true sale aspect of the transaction on behalf of the securityholders. A major concern of the securityholders is that the trust maintains a security interest in the underlying assets and that the entity status of the trust remains intact. The trustee is additionally concerned that the governing documents do not unnecessarily burden the transaction parties in performing their duties and responsibilities.

Operational Errors

Because of the complexities of an asset-backed securitization, the trustee is at greater risk of an operational error than on a typical capital markets transaction.

---

[5] This can be further exasperated when, as is the case in the majority of transactions, the servicing fees are calculated as percentage of the declining balance of the assets over time. Unfortunately, the costs for servicing the assets are not declining over time.

Operational errors may include an incorrect or missed distribution, misapplication of funds between transaction participants, incorrect investment of funds, lost collateral documentation, and the untimely or missed notification of a significant event.

On most asset-backed securitizations, the trustee receives distribution information from the servicer as part of the servicer's monthly report. An incorrect distribution may cause negative arbitrage causing shortages in funds to cover debt service for the expected life of the security. Unless the distributions are carefully calculated by the servicer, a mistake may not be identified immediately which could result in a significant claim against the trust.

If the income earned on invested cash is used to support the transaction's flow of funds, it becomes critical that the trustee invest the funds correctly. If the funds are not invested in a timely manner by the trustee, the payments to the underlying securityholders may be affected. Furthermore, if the trustee invests funds outside the acceptable investment criteria of the transaction, the trustee could expose the trust to investment losses.

To maintain the security interest in many asset-backed securitizations, the servicer is required to file UCC continuation statements and safekeep evidence of security title (notes, mortgages, titles, etc.). If there is a lapse in a UCC continuation filing, it is conceivable that the lien priority of the security may be lost or reduced. If the documented evidence of title or security interest is lost or misplaced, the obligor could petition a court to eliminate the indebtedness.

The trustee disseminates, as required under the governing documents, all pertinent information that it may acquire regarding the underlying assets, servicer[6] or other matters having a material effect on the investors. If the trustee does not forward beneficial information to the investors, that gives the investors notice to take action which may benefit them, then the trustee may be held accountable.

Many of the risks the trustee must address on an asset-backed securitization could cause severe economical hardship for the trustee.

TRUSTEE QUALIFICATIONS

Trustee qualifications are very stringent in the asset-backed market and contribute to the relative small number of market participants. Trustees must meet certain regulatory qualifications and minimum capitalization requirements. Qualified trustees must also have a well-seasoned and trained staff with securitization experience and knowledge of a variety of asset types and transaction structures. Additionally, trustees must invest significantly in operations processes and systems technology to process these complicated transactions. Successful trustees must also be able to demonstrate a commitment to the trust business that can be measured by the management resources and control infrastructure dedicated to asset-backed securitizations.

---

[6] The trustee is normally required to receive quarterly financials and annual audit reports from the servicer.

Regulatory and Capitalization Requirements

Depending on the bank charter and state domicile of the trustee, the trustee may be regulated by a number of agencies including, but not limited to, the appropriate state banking authority, FDIC, Federal Reserve, and The Office of the Controller of the Currency. Additionally, the Trust Indenture Act of 1939 ("TIA"), as amended, establishes requirements for trustees of most public offerings in excess of $10,000,000. These requirements cover minimum net worth of trustees, standard of care limits, conflict of interest rules, and regulatory reporting requirements. Since most asset-backed securitizations are structured such that the investor is holding certificates of interests in the underlying assets, as opposed to debt, they are generally exempt from the TIA. Although it may not be a legal requirement, trustees may still be required to meet the TIA requirements.

The combined capital and surplus requirements of the trustee by the TIA are set at a very minimal amount of $150,000. Many transaction structures of an asset-backed securitizations have a much more restrictive capital requirement of $50,000,000 or greater. Additionally, many transaction structures require the trustee to maintain a principal office location in New York City.[7]

Staffing Requirements

Because of the high degree of specialization and complexity associated with the asset-backed securitization industry, proper staffing by the trustee is a critical success factor for ongoing administration of the transaction. Qualified trustees should have experienced account managers with a proven record of administering similar structured transactions and a familiarity of the specific asset type. Additionally, the ongoing administration of the transaction should be performed by trust officers who have received significant training in trust administration, trust banking systems, ethical business practices and customer service.

If the trustee is performing additional functions (tax reporting agent, bond calculation agent, backup servicer, etc.) it is also important that the trustee staff demonstrate an appropriate amount of expertise in each of those areas.

Operations and Technology

Providing trust services to the asset-backed securitization market is a demanding operational and technological proposition. Large scale trustee participants have an immense operational staff to handle the intricate securities processing requirements of asset-backed transactions. This includes providing registrar and bond recordkeeping services, funds disbursements, and document custodian services.

Sophisticated computer systems are required to support the trustee in providing services to asset-backed marketplace. The funds disbursement systems must be able to process thousands of simultaneous transactions for the proper distribution of funds on the bond distribution date. The trustee must have links to all major

---

[7] Some asset-backed securitizations have required the trustee to maintain offices in California.

clearing organizations (CEDEL, Euroclear, DTC, PTC, etc.) to ensure the swift movement of moneys to the correct corresponding entities. Additionally, significant technological resources are needed to support the tickler system that computerizes many of the administrative follow-up items required of the trustee. Advanced technology, including imaging, is required to support the evolving document custody process, while a flexible technology architecture is needed to handle the complexities associated with the tax reporting and bond payment calculation agent functions. Since many of these services and products are now required to be offered online or via the Internet, trustees need to maintain up-to-date technologies.

Commitment to Trust Business

Because of the staffing, operational, and technological commitments, coupled with a steady declining pricing environment, many trustees have decided to exit the corporate trust business. The remaining trust entities must continue to invest in superior technology and a knowledgeable staff to remain viable market participants. Additionally, to minimize risk to themselves and ensure appropriate service to clients, the trustee must have a significant control and management oversight infrastructure. This includes appropriate transaction acceptance procedures and ongoing self assessment and deal review procedures. Trustees who are committed to the asset-backed securitization sector will continue to invest significant resources and examine ways to institute best practices across all trust business functions.

Index